BR North of the Border

BR North of the Border

L.A.NIXON & P.J.ROBINSON

LONDON

IAN ALLAN LTD

Contents

Introduction

Cover: No 37.022 seen in typical highland scenery with the 16.36 Glasgow–Fort William near Crianlarich on 6 May 1982. *Mrs D. A. Robinson*

First published 1983

ISBN 0 7110 1327 6

Published by Ian Allan Ltd, Shepperton, Surrey; and printed by Ian Allan Printing Ltd at their works at Coombelands in Runnymede, England

Of the five regions of British Rail it is the Scottish which serves the largest geographical area and includes the greatest diversity of scenery. The highest mountains, the largest expanses of inland water, the longest coastline are tempered by the extremes of Scottish weather. The relatively mild climate of the south-west contrasts markedly the rigours of the Grampian winter and the gales of the Far North. Demographic variations are equally varied, ranging from the sparsely populated north-west to the industrialised conurbations of the Central Lowlands. Not surprisingly these factors combined to mould a somewhat unique railway development, and a century later, to influence rationalisation. In compiling this album we offer a present day reflection of this amazing variety.

The overwhelming impression gained in selecting the pictures and in writing the captions, is of sadness at the way our unique railway heritage has been largely lost. Although the transfer of both freight and passenger traffic from rail to road and has been gradual, there seems to have been little attempt by politicians and professional railwaymen alike to reverse, or even check, this trend. The expansion of the trunk road network at the expense of the railways is now irreversible, particularly when employment statistics are considered. Today hundreds of thousands of people derive employment from road transport whereas only about 160,000 are employed by British Rail. On rational economic and ecological grounds rail borne traffic is both cheaper and healthier than road haulage. More importantly there is no comparison on humanitarian grounds between the safety record of the railways and the tragic slaughter which is phlegmatically tolerated on the road system.

North of the Border the reduction in rail traffic has already lost for ever such arteries as the Port Road, the Waverley route and the superbly aligned Stanley Junction to Kinnaber Junction line, along with countless rural branches. Other lines are now 'basic' railways with vandalised unstaffed stations and worn out rolling stock. Scottish railway eccentricities such as the annual seed potato traffic to Eastern England and whisky trains to and from the distilleries of Speyside are lost to the roads for ever.

However the electrified Glasgow suburban system, the West Coast main line to Carlisle, the highly popular Edinburgh to Glasgow push-pull Mk 3 stock services and the introduction of HSTs through to Aberdeen offer Scots the very best of modern rail operation and design. On the freight side both Freightliners and Speedlink air-braked services carry significant traffic to and from the industrial centres and merry-go-round coal operations feed the Forth-Clyde valley power stations.

Fortunately it is still possible to take a relaxed view of the beautiful Scottish scenery through the carriage window on routes such as those to Kyle, Stranraer, Oban and the Far North. Hopefully Scots will adopt the same grit and determination to retain these services as was evident in the successful lobby to save Ravenscraig.

We have concentrated on showing Scotland's railways to advantage which has resulted in a larger proportion of pictures in scenic rather than industrial locations. We hope that readers will agree that this slight imbalance makes for a more attractive album of railways North of the Border.

L. A. Nixon & P. J. Robinson
Hathersage
North Shields
February 1983

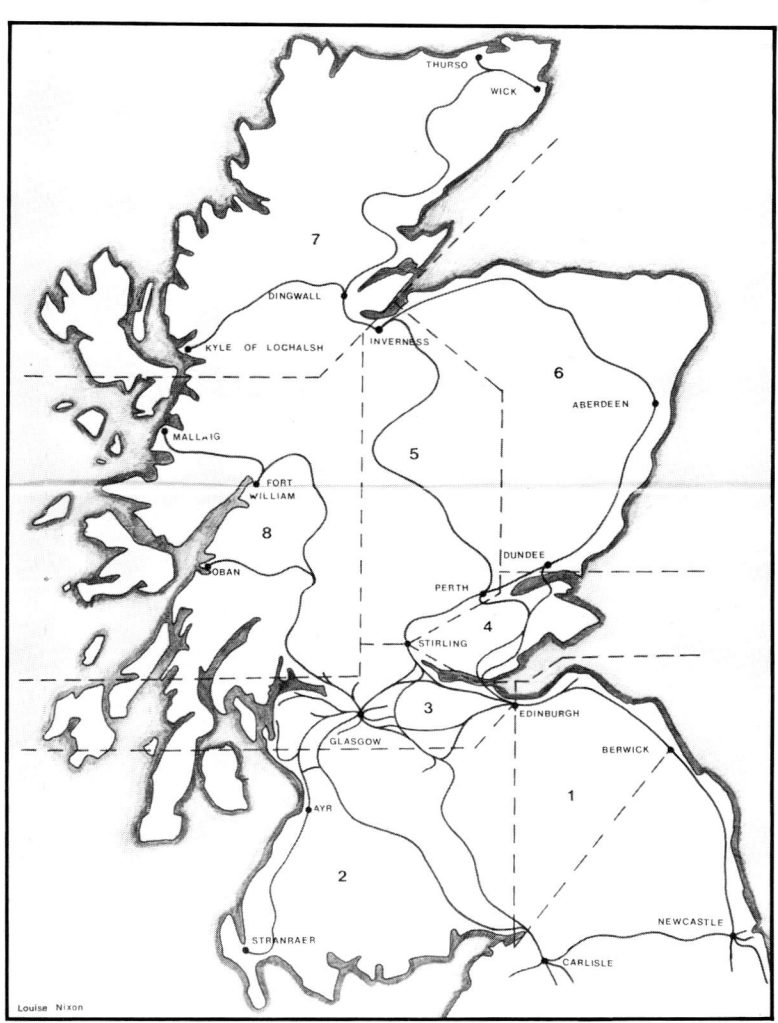

Louise Nixon

Left: Map of Scotland. 1 South-east Scotland; 2 South-west Scotland; 3 The Lowlands; 4 Fife; 5 Stirling to Inverness; 6 North-east Scotland; 7 The Far North; 8 The West Highland.

South-east Scotland

The rail network in this area has been reduced to the arterial East Coast main line from Edinburgh to Berwick with only one remaining branch from Drem to North Berwick — the Waverley Route from Edinburgh to Carlisle having been tragically closed in 1969. Both traversed a variety of beautiful scenery and the Edinburgh-Berwick stretch is arguably the most scenic Inter-City line on BR, initially passing through the coastal coal mining area of East Lothian, followed by the rolling pastoral Border hills and finishing with the dramatic run along the Berwickshire cliff tops before crossing the Border at Marshall Meadows, just north of Berwick. For the 16 years, from 1963-78, the express passenger services were dominated by the visually and audibly magnificent 'Deltic' 3,300hp diesel locomotives, giving way to the popular standard HST 125mph train sets in 1979. Since dieselisation Classes 40, 46 and 47 have played supporting roles on secondary passenger duties with Classes 37 and 40 monopolising freight.

Below: Although hardly looking a candidate for the scrap heap No 55.018 *Ballymoss* was withdrawn only two days after this picture was taken of the Sunday 11.25 Edinburgh-Plymouth passing Houndwood on 11 October 1981. In fact *Ballymoss* had quite a noteworthy day which started by rescuing its train from within Carlton Hill tunnel due to the failure of the Class 47 bringing the stock from Craigentinny. This resulted in a 15min late departure which had been virtually recovered when it passed the photographer 44 miles from Edinburgh. It continued to gain time, actually arriving in Newcastle over 15min early, no doubt to the delight of the 'Deltic' fans on board.   *PJR*

Left: Approaching Edinburgh from the east is Class 47 No 47.430, in charge of the 08.40 York-Aberdeen, racing past Class 26 No 26.002 awaiting the release signal from Blindwells opencast site with a MGR coal train for Cockenzie power station — less than a mile away on the north side of the main line, 17 June 1982. *PJR*

Below: The $4\frac{1}{2}$-mile branch from Drem to North Berwick is used principally by commuters with some day trippers to the coast in the opposite direction. For this traffic an infrequent DMU service is provided mainly to and from Haymarket. Here the 11.03 North Berwick-Haymarket is seen approaching Drem formed of the usual three-car set, strengthened by the addition of a single unit for Christmas shoppers on 4 December 1982. *PJR*

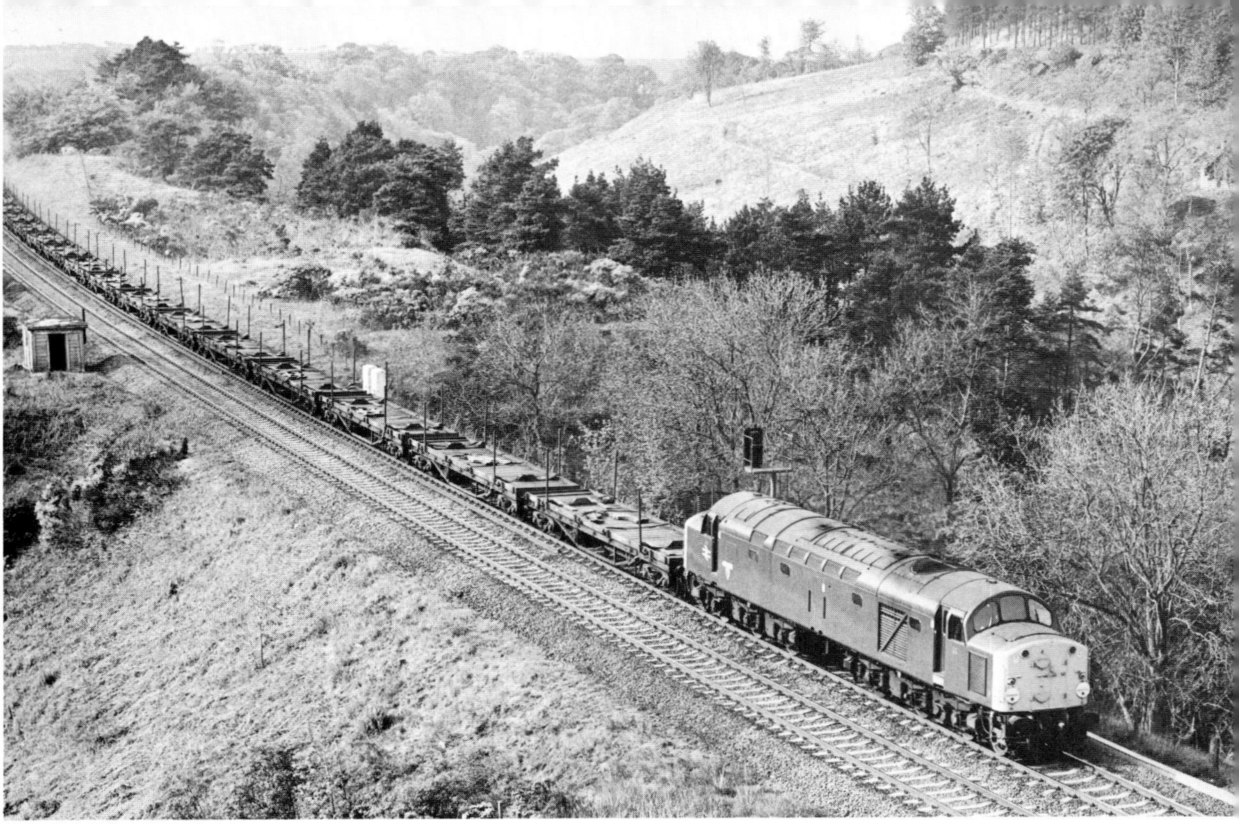

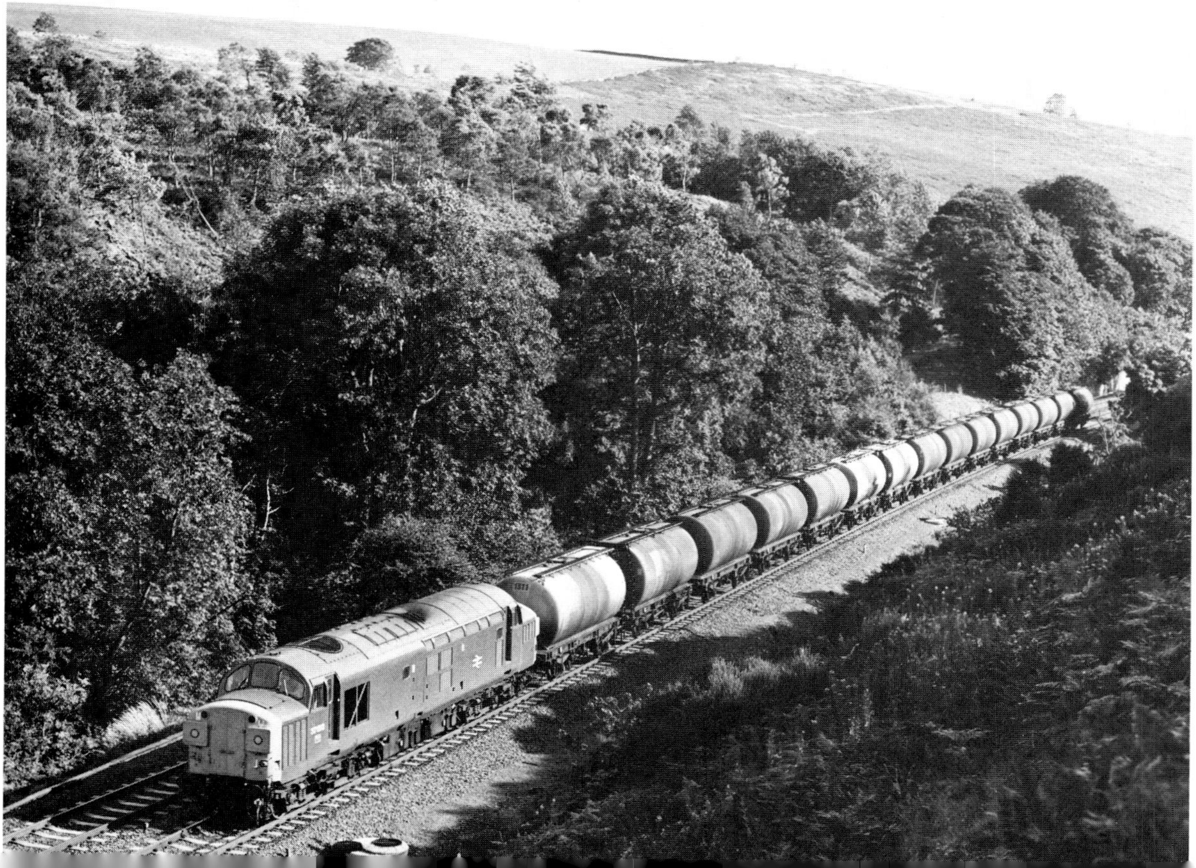

Left: After a level run to Dunbar the East Coast main line starts to climb above the sea and turns inland at Cockburnspath at 1 in 96, up a narrow wooded valley towards Grantshouse summit. Here Class 40 No 40.036 is about one-mile up the valley with a long train of empty steel pipe carrying wagons. The pipes are usually coated at Leith and transported by rail from BSC Hartlepool, where they are rolled. *PJR*

Below left: Near the summit of the climb, the line becomes very enclosed at Penmansheil. Here Class 37 No 37.013 is starting the descent with the Jarrow-Leith oil tanks on 6 September 1980. *PJR*

Right: The climb up the narrowing valley from Cockburnspath culminated in the ill-fated Penmansheil tunnel which collapsed in March 1979 during excavations to lower the floor level, so as to permit the passage of 8ft 6in Freightliner containers. At the time one line had been lifted and single line working was in force. The collapse entombed two workmen whose bodies could not be recovered — a monument to their memory now stands high above the sealed off tunnel. This accident closed the main line until August 1979 during which period passenger traffic was either diverted from Newcastle to Carlisle, reaching Edinburgh via Carstairs, or passengers were ferried by bus between Berwick and Dunbar. Both 'solutions' extended journey times by about 90min. The instability of the rock necessitated the substitution of a cutting blasted through the hillside on the alignment of the A1 road which was itself re-aligned west of the new railway. This alteration had the effect of producing several new locations for the railway photographer. Here Class 40 No 40.164 approaches the new deviation, working flat out with 1E86, the 07.34 Glasgow-Scarborough additional on 18 July 1981. *PJR*

Below: Class 37 No 37.161 from Thornaby TMD enjoys a rare 'fling' on passenger work as it races downhill towards Cockburnspath with 1S99, the 12.00 Scarborough-Glasgow additional on 29 July 1978. *PJR*

Left: A superb view of southbound trains can now be enjoyed from the hillside above the sealed Penmansheil tunnel. Here 'Deltic' No 55.008 *The Green Howards* is negotiating the new alignment with the 09.50 Edinburgh-Plymouth on 18 April 1981. This working was the last full load diagram for a 'Deltic', the first coach usually being packed with 'Deltic' fans savouring the distinctive sound and smell at the eleventh hour. At York a Class 47/4 will take over, enabling No 55.008 to return to Edinburgh with the corresponding Plymouth-Edinburgh train. *PJR*

Right: Making a stirring noise Class 55 No 55.013 *The Black Watch* sweeps round the curve past the loops at Grantshouse summit at the head of the 07.36 Plymouth-Edinburgh on Good Friday, 17 April 1981. *PJR*

Below: Class 55 No 55.011 *Royal Northumberland Fusilier* leaves the northern end of the Penmansheil deviation with a down sleeping car train on 18 July 1981. The original alignment entered the tunnel at the grassy mound which can be seen near the rear of the train. The effect of blasting the new cutting is clearly visible. *PJR*

11

Above: The LNER 'London 350 Miles' sign must be of pure academic interest to the crew and passengers of the 17.10 Edinburgh-Berwick stopping train, seen here pottering downhill near Houndwood behind ex-works Class 25 No 25.237 on 17 July 1977. From Grantshouse the line traverses the rolling hills of the pastoral Border countryside whose appearance changes very noticeably from season to season. *PJR*

Below: Class 45 No 45.125 provides very unusual power for the 11.40 Dundee-Kings Cross, coasting downhill round the scenic curve at Houndwood on 10 June 1978. *PJR*

Top: The harvested cornfields are a mellow golden colour as brand new HST set No 254 018, forming the 11.10 Edinburgh-Kings Cross, speeds towards the coast past Horn Burn on a blustery 6 October 1978. *PJR*

Above: At sunset on a wild December day a southbound HST scurries along the coast near Innerwick, silhouetted against an angry sky. *PJR*

Right: The inflexibility of HST train sets has resulted in considerable numbers of locomotive hauled additionals at peak holiday times. While 'Deltics' worked several of these vacuum brake, steam heated trains formed of Mk 1 stock, the majority were powered by the 138-ton giants of Class 46, all the survivors of which were transferred to Gateshead TMD during 1980/81. Here the only named Class 46, No 46.026 *The Leicestershire & Derbyshire Yeomanry*, speeds through verdant spring cornfields at Horn Burn with the 13.25 Edinburgh-Kings Cross additional on a beautiful late spring day, 25 May 1981. *PJR*

Below: 'Peak' Class 45 locomotives are infrequent visitors north of Newcastle since the introduction of ETH Mk 2 stock on the Edinburgh-Plymouth trains. Here split indicator No 45.013 is seen accelerating away from Grantshouse summit on 18 September 1976 past the now demolished signalbox. At this time the train was still formed of dual heated Mk 1 and 2 stock. *PJR*

Above: Immediately after passing the site of the erstwhile Burnmouth station southbound trains reach the clifftops along which they run for the next six miles to Berwick upon Tweed. In this picture Class 31 No 31.162 of Finsbury Park TMD is extremely unusual power for the 17.10 Edinburgh-Newcastle stopping train on 18 July 1978. *PJR*

Below: It is no longer possible to stand at Peelwalls to listen for several minutes to the rise and fall of a racing 'Deltic' as it speeds downhill from Reston to finally burst forth from the woods in a cacophony of noise. From here trains attack the brief rise to Ayton before swooping down to the clifftops at Burnmouth. Magnificent in its newly restored green livery 'Deltic' No 55.002 *King's Own Yorkshire Light Infantry* is a welcome surprise as it emerges from the trees in charge of the 09.50 Edinburgh-Plymouth on the drowsy mid-summer morning of 10 June 1981. *PJR*

Above: Although a portent for the future the provision of No 55.003 *Meld* to power this returning Kings Cross-Edinburgh return football special after the 1977 Wembley England v Scotland fixture was very unusual as 'Deltics' could not usually be spared for such duties. However *Meld* was a welcome surprise racing north along the cliffs on the cloudless Sunday afternoon with 10 Mk 1 coaches, forming the 1F51 10.15 Kings Cross-Edinburgh Footex. *PJR*

Below: Against a dramatic background of jagged cliffs 'Deltic' No 55.022 *Royal Scots Grey* roars northwards, at the head of an Anglo-Scottish express, past Lamberton with the North Sea in an uncharacteristically calm mood in the spring of 1981. *PJR*

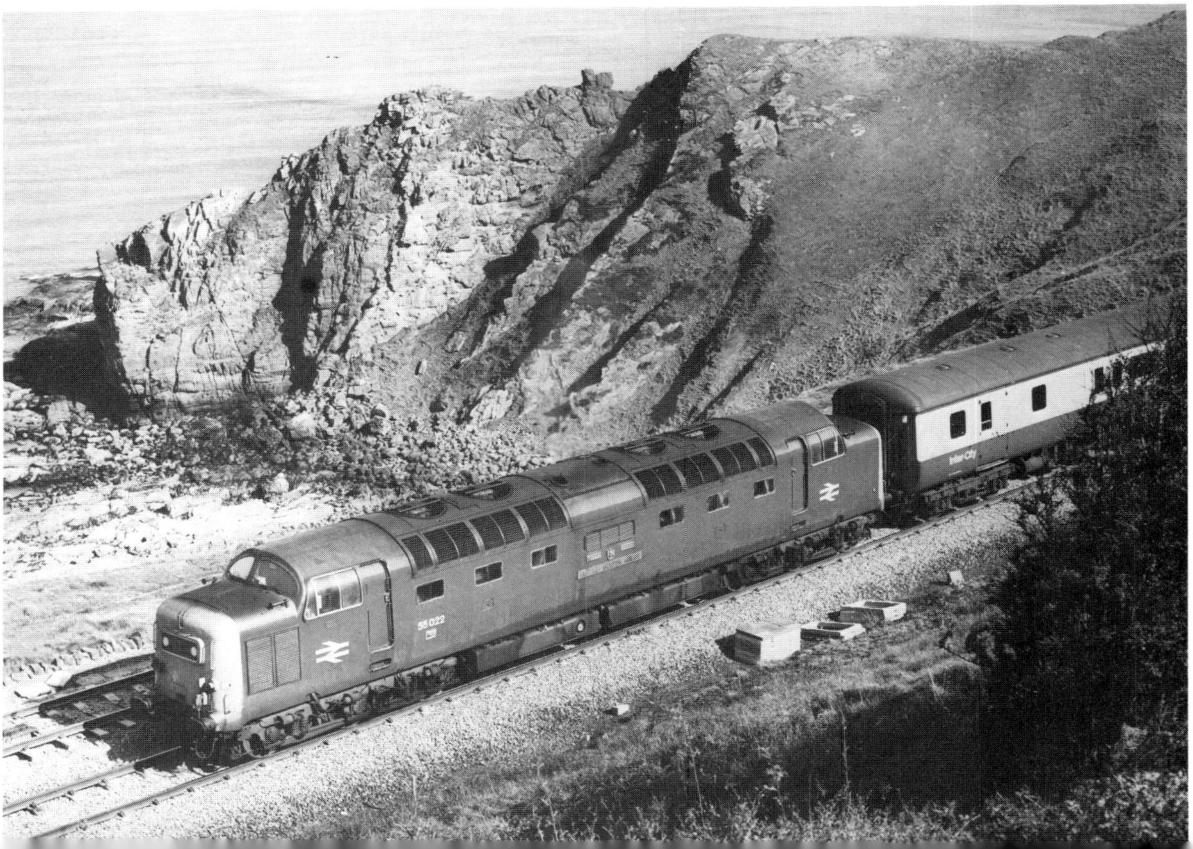

This picture: Still rostered for a Class 40 at the time of writing (December 1982) the daily Haverton Hill–Leith train of ICI ammonia tanks makes a stirring audio-visual spectacle as it pounds uphill from Berwick to Grantshouse. In this view immaculate Haymarket-based No 40.164 is working at full power as it 'whistles' along the cliffs on the hazy afternoon of 14 March 1979. *PJR*

The Waverley Route

Although the North British Railway's Waverley route from Carlisle to Edinburgh was closed in 1969 we could not resist the inclusion of a small vignette as a memento of this fascinating and much mourned railway. Probably its most note worthy feature was the isolated railway village of Riccarton Junction where the meandering Border Counties branch trailed in from Hexham. This small railway community of about 30 houses was inaccessible by road, the railway being the only lifeline. In an emergency a doctor would be rushed out from Hawick on a light engine. Distinguished in steam days for the variety of motive power, this trend continued into the diesel age as our small selection shows.

Below: At the northern extremity of the Waverley route 'Clayton' Class 17 No D8583 leaves Lady Victoria colliery at Newtongrange for the short run to Millerhill yard on 9 April 1970. At that time this was the only traffic south of Millerhill, operated on the one engine in steam system which explains the complete absence of signalling. *LAN*

Bottom: Class 17s Nos D8565 and D8566 along with a Class 40, No D398, provide 'super power' for a Carlisle-Millerhill freight, seen here near Stow on 3 September 1966. *LAN*

Left: The last daytime passenger train over the Waverley route was an RCTS railtour from Leeds to Edinburgh via Carlisle, returning via Berwick on 5 January 1969. An inspired move was the provision of an immaculate 'Deltic', No 55.007 *Pinza*, to haul the train throughout. This picture shows the excursion restarting from Riccarton Junction after a 'wake' on the platform enlivened by a dusting of snow. *PJR*

Below: Riccarton Junction was three-quarters of the way up the 10-mile northbound climb at 1 in 75 from Newcastleton to Whitrope through bleak windswept hills. Here Class 40 No D285 ambles downhill amidst the desolate fells about $\frac{1}{2}$-mile south of Riccarton with an Edinburgh-Carlisle all stations stopping train in the summer of 1965. By this date most of the 'village' had been demolished but one or two grey stone cottages can be seen in the distance at the top right. *PJR*

South-west Scotland

This section embraces the more southerly parts of the former Glasgow & South Western Railway, from Kilmarnock to Gretna and through Ayr to Stranraer, along with the prestigious Caledonian trunk route south of Carstairs to Carlisle. The 25kV electrified line from Glasgow to Carlisle is, with the possible exception of Edinburgh to Glasgow, the most intensively used Scottish Inter-City route. These days a journey through the industrial suburbs of Glasgow and Motherwell, the sweeping broad valleys of the upper Clyde and over Beattock summit to the rolling farmlands of Dumfriesshire is completed in a little over one hour, a far cry from the days of steam and early dieselisation. The lumbering performances of overworked Class 40s on 14-coach trains gave way in the early 1970s to the improved services provided by Class 50s in tandem, which were themselves soon ousted by electric traction. By comparison trains over the GS&W are infrequent and leisurely, appropriate perhaps to the essentially rural communities they serve. Ayr to Stranraer survives as the only remaining realistic route to Northern Ireland since the closure of the direct line from Carlisle through Castle Douglas in 1965. The circuitous journey now necessary for passengers to and from destinations south of the Border is at least compensated by some of the finest scenery in southern Scotland. The section between Girvan and Challoch Junction is of particular interest. From Girvan the line climbs high above the Firth of Clyde at a punitive 1 in 54 to a summit at Pinmore tunnel, followed by an equally sharp descent to Pinwherry. From Barrhill the route snakes across wild and desolate moorland,

Below: Gretna Junction to Annan is the southernmost single line section of the GSW main line. Part can just be discerned beyond the rear coach in this photograph at Annan of No 47.485 with the 10.20 Nottingham-Glasgow (Central) on 28 August 1980. Note the BR totem station sign at the top left. *LAN*

reminiscent of Caithness scenery at the other end of the country.

Ayr is the focal point of the region and is the natural distribution centre by sea and rail for the Ayrshire coalfield which continues to generate much of the freight traffic of the area. Ayr is also at the southern extremity of a quite intensive commuter service to Clydeside, presently provided by an ageing DMU fleet. The economic case for the extension of the 25kV network to the Ayrshire coast must be sound even if the GS&W main line south of Kilmarnock has ultimately to be sacrificed at the altar of profitable railway operation.

Below and bottom: The rolling hill scenery which typifies southern Scotland is clearly evident in these panoramic views of the Glasgow & South Western main line near Drumlanrigg. (Below) Class 25 No 25.218 powers the five coach 08.40 Carlisle-Glasgow on 9 April 1982 while exactly one week later (Bottom) Class 47 No 47.501 with the 13.15 Stranraer-Euston, was photographed heading south at almost the same location. *LAN*

Above: Class 47/4 No 47.445 passes Bank
Junction west of New Cumnock with the
10.20 Nottingham-Glasgow (Central) on
29 August 1981. The signalbox is now rarely
opened following the closure of the collieries
at Knockshinnoch at the end of the two-mile
branch seen diverging to the right. Vandalism
is evidently a problem even in this relatively
rural part of Ayrshire since the signalbox
windows are well protected with heavy duty
wire mesh netting. *LAN*

Right: The Glasgow & South Western main
line becomes an important alternative route
when the Caledonian line is closed due to an
accident or engineering work. Here a
Birmingham-Glasgow express with two
Class 50s in charge (No D436 leading)
approaches Sanquhar on 9 June 1972.
John Cooper-Smith

Above: For many years 'Peaks' and Class 40s were regular performers north of the border on the St Pancras-Glasgow, and latterly Nottingham-Glasgow services. In 1980 following a series of derailment incidents, locomotives of 1Co-Co1 wheel arrangement were banned from Glasgow Central and today the usual motive power is the ubiquitous Class 47. Here No 47.482 nears Mennock with the 10.20 Nottingham-Glasgow on 25 August 1981. *LAN*

Below: In 1966 Ayr was one of the last refuges of the Hughes 'Crab' 2-6-0 steam locomotives. At that time trip workings to the local collieries were worked 'cox and box' with Class 25 and Class 20 diesel-electrics and scenes such as this at Annbank Junction were commonplace. Class 25 No D7616 and tender first 'Crab' No 42803 take the freight only line to Mauchline Junction with a string of coal empties for Barony Colliery on 30 August 1966. *LAN*

This picture: An unusually clean pair of 'Choppers' Class 20 Nos 20.125 and 20.002 take a string of empty wagons out of the docks area at Ayr on 31 August 1979. *LAN*

Right: English Electric 1,000hp Class 20 No 20.080 and the Ayr breakdown train, comprising several interesting items of departmental stock, attend to a derailed tank wagon at Newton-on-Ayr early in the morning of 26 August 1981. Note the firemen's hoses taken under the track to the site of the accident. Heads of Ayr is clearly visible across the bay, once on the alternative coastline route to Girvan. *LAN*

Below: After a shower of rain, the drying platforms of Ayr station, make interesting foreground patterns as a pair of Class 20s, Nos 20.116 and 20.201, rattle through with a northbound van train on 31 August 1979. *LAN*

Above and below: Between New Luce, Glenwhilly and Barrhill the Stranraer line traverses some of the most open and desolate scenery in all Scotland; indeed in parts it rivals the infamous Rannoch Moor of the West Highland line. These photographs show Class 40 No 40.063 at work near Glenwhilly on the morning of 27 August 1981. In the scene above the 'Whistler' heads for Stranraer at 07.00 with a train of long welded rail while below she is seen some four hours later returning north with a trivial load of four vans. *LAN*

Left: Class 25 No 25.050 runs round a freight train which it had earlier brought into the now disused Stranraer Town station on 23 August 1980. As part of the Portpatrick & Wigtown Joint Railway the line once extended beyond the bridge to Colfin and to a terminus at Portpatrick. Passenger services to Portpatrick were withdrawn on 6 February 1950. *LAN*

Below: BRCW Type 2 No 27.212 heads the summer only 13.43 Kilmarnock-Stranraer through superb scenery south of Barrhill on 27 August 1981. The train is traversing the section of line which was washed away during severe thunderstorms on 27 July 1980 when earthworks were severley breached in two places, isolating a Class 47 and her train for three days. *LAN*

Above: Class 25 No 25.224 takes a featherweight pick up freight, comprising three four-wheeled vans, down the 1 in 54 from Pinmore summit into Girvan on 28 August 1981. In good weather passengers travelling over this section of the Stranraer line enjoy magnificent views of the Forth of Clyde and the steep cliffs of the tiny island landmark of Ailsa Craig. *LAN*

Below: Flat out on the now singled Girvan-Maybole line near Killochan Castle at Old Dailly is Class 27 No 27.041 with the six-coach summer only 10.36 Stranraer-Kilmarnock on 26 August 1981. *LAN*

West Coast main line

The essence of WCML travel

Today: The late 1970s and early 1980s typified by Class No 87.001 *Royal Scot* and Mk 3 stock forming the 12.45 Euston-Glasgow nears Greskine on 24 July 1982. *Tomorrow:* The everyday service of the late 1980s and 1990s will probably be a development of the Advanced Passenger Train. Experimental unit No 370.001, undergoing trials, passes No 40.165 in the loop at Beattock on 30 July 1979. *PJR*

Below and bottom: Two contrasting views of Freightliner operation on the WCML north of Carlisle. (Below) At Crawford Class 87 No 87.006 *City of Glasgow* pilots Class 86 No 86.318 northbound with a full pay load on 16 April 1981. Double-headed electric locomotives are now diagrammed for freightliners since in adverse conditions adhesion problems often reduce single locomotives to walking speed on Beattock bank. (Bottom) Diverted from the East Coast route because of the Penmanshiel tunnel disaster, Class 37s Nos 37.219 and 37.173 heads a Parkeston-Glasgow service on 30 July 1979. *LAN/PJR*

Above: In the few years between the end of steam and the electrification of the Glasgow-Carlisle main line, services were accelerated by the rather costly expedient of double-heading the principal expresses with English Electric Class 50s. In this scene Nos D412 and D410, (later renumbered and named 50.012 *Benbow* and 50.010 *Monarch*), round the curves near Abington with an evening Glasgow-Birmingham express on 4 June 1970. *John Cooper-Smith*

Below: With 16 coaches in tow Class 81 No 81.014 hustles through Crawford with the Mondays only Derby-Glasgow empty stock train on 30 July 1979. The ascent of Beattock must have been quite a proposition for the ageing electric locomotive. *PJR*

Left: A scene which has since changed beyond recognition. An unidentified Class 50 negotiates the interesting trackwork at Strawfrank Junction, Carstairs at the head of an up Freightliner late in the evening of 5 June 1972. *John Cooper-Smith*

Top right: In 1982 Paddington was probably the most unusual destination of an up train on the former Caledonian main line. Heading for the Western Region Class 86 No 86.219 *Pheonix* crosses Harthope viaduct and the A74 trunk road with the combined 13.26 ex-Edinburgh and the 13.43 ex-Glasgow on 24 July 1982. *PJR*

Below right: Unfamiliar surroundings for a 'Deltic'. Green-liveried No 55.002 *Kings Own Yorkshire Light Infantry* romps up Beattock with an enthusiasts Kings Cross-Edinburgh excursion on 25 April 1981. The train was to have travelled north from Leeds over the S&C but due to blockage by snow it was diverted via Shap. *PJR*

Below: A group of American tourists are treated to the delights of the ascent of Beattock as they sit back in the comfort of the all first class accommodation of 1Z25, a Holyhead to Edinburgh and Glasgow charter, on 24 July 1982. Class 86 No 86.213 *Lancashire Witch* provides the motive power. *PJR*

Left: Since the closure of the Waverley route in 1969 the Carstairs-Edinburgh line has assumed a more important role in Anglo-Scottish rail services. It is now common practice for down expresses to be divided at Carstairs for Edinburgh and Glasgow destinations. In this scene to the north of Carstairs two young enthusiasts lean out of the leading coach of the 14.40 ex-Edinburgh to discover the identity of the locomotive which will take them on the next stage of their journey south to Manchester Victoria. Class 87 No 87.006 *City of Glasgow* approaches with the 15.02 Glasgow portion while Class 47 No 47.709 *The Lord Provost* waits to propel the Edinburgh portion on to the back on 17 April 1982. *LAN*

Above right: The terminus at Lanark is reached by a short two-mile branch from Lanark Junction situated on the WCML to the west of Carstairs. The town enjoys an excellent interval service of no fewer than 31 weekly departures to and arrivals from Glasgow (Central). However, business seems to be anything but brisk for the 25kV Class 303 EMU forming the 15.26 service to Glasgow on 19 April 1979. *LAN*

Below right: Over the years much has been written about the famous banks of the West Coast route — Shap and Beattock. Present day passengers may be totally unaware of their existence since trains travel up the banks as fast as they go down. Not so for drivers of freight trains — northbound, Beattock is still 10 gruelling miles at a ruling gradient of 1 in 74. Here Class 83 No 83.013 and Class 86 No 86.024 prepare to begin the climb as they pull out of the loop and on to the main line at Beattock with a tank train on 2 August 1979. Until recently two locomotives, usually Class 20s manned by Carstairs crews, were based at Beattock for banking duties. *PJR*

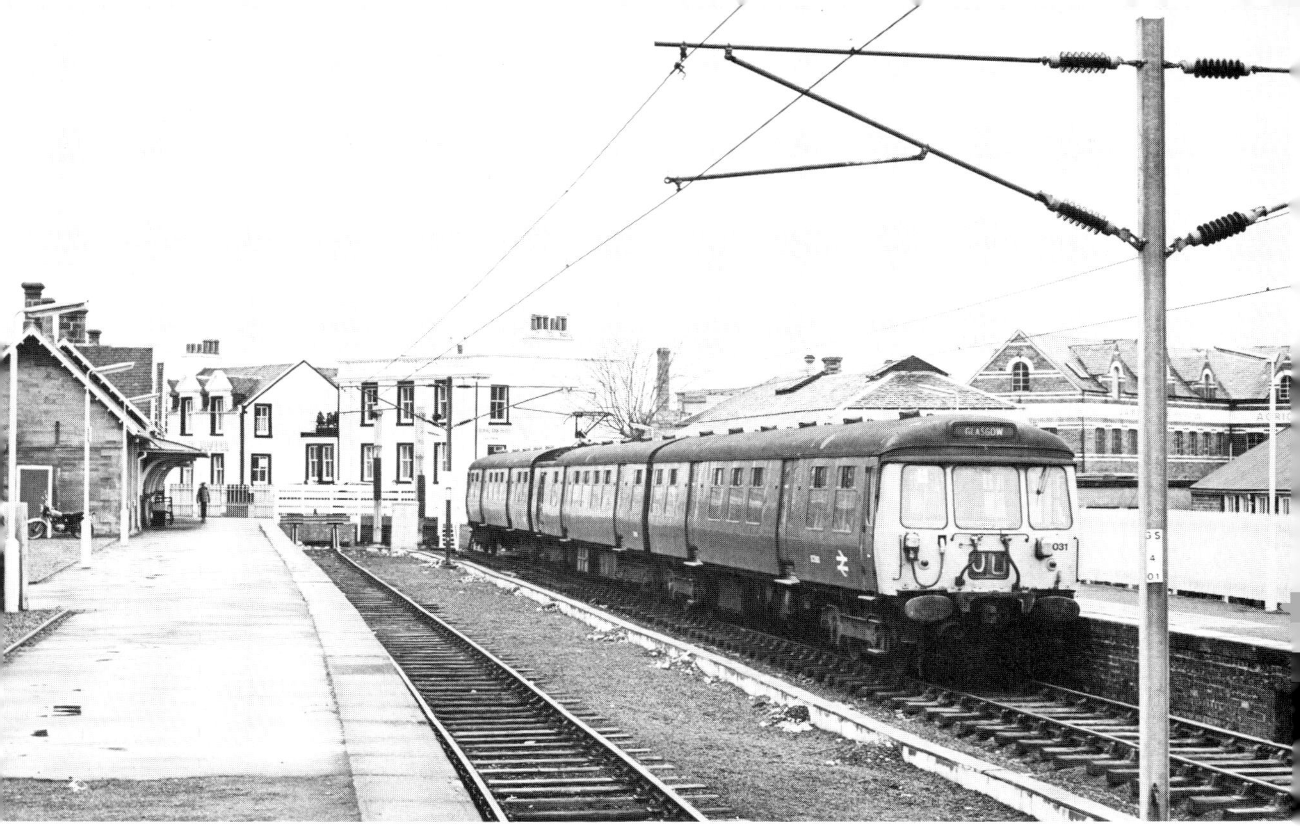
GLASGOW
031

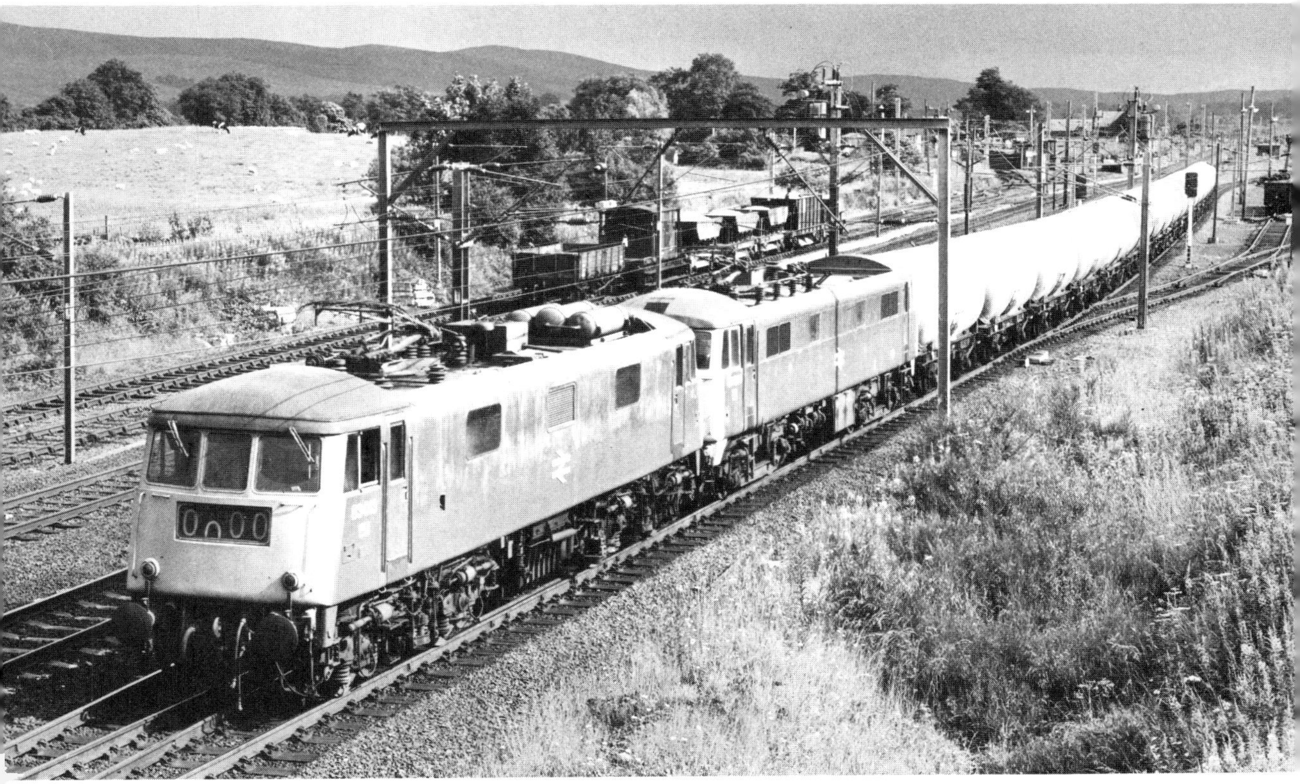

Above: A shutter speed of 1/1,000 second was required to freeze the movement of No 86.228 *Vulcan Heritage* travelling at 90mph *up* Beattock bank near Harthope with the 13.45 Liverpool-Edinburgh on 25 April 1981. A train consist of four Mk 1 coaches is unusual, arising no doubt from the extreme winter weather south of the Border on that date. *PJR*

Below: English Electric Type 1 No 20.099 trundles down the West Coast main line near Crawford at a sedate 40mph with a ballast train bound for Beattock on 9 April 1982. Just visible at the rear of the train is another Class 20 providing valuable banking assistance. *David Nixon*

The Lowlands

This industrial heartland of Scotland is still served by a comprehensive rail network centred on the two great cities of Edinburgh and Glasgow and the connecting routes. Passenger suburban services to the Edinburgh dormitories in Fife and the Lothians are worked by a combination of DMU and diesel hauled services, whilst Glasgow commuters from Clydeside and the Clyde Valley have the benefit of a 25kV overhead electric network upon which the attractive Gresley bogied Class 303 'Blue trains' are gradually being superseded by the current standard BR units. There are numerous flows of full trainload freight traffic, including oil and chemical products, coal, iron ore, shale spoil, grain and various steel pipes. Wagon load traffic for Scottish destinations is disseminated from the large marshalling yards at Millerhill (Edinburgh) and Mossend (Glasgow). Similarly wagon loads from the various centres in Scotland for English destinations are sorted into trainloads for the South. The rundown in wagon load traffic and the growth of the Speedlink Air Braked trains has dramatically reduced the throughput of these huge marshalling yards which are now relics of a bygone age.

Although this area embraces a wealth of railway interest, it is scenically rather mundane with only one or two bright spots.

Below: Although the short branch from Craigentinny to Leith handles a large volume of rail traffic by today's standards, Leith is a shadow of its former self. Here on 14 June 1982 No 37.163 negotiates the single track branch, passing through desolate acres of lifted railway sidings with the regular mid afternoon train of oil tanks for Teesside. Across the Firth of Forth can be seen the Fife coast around Kinghorn. *PJR*

Right: In this wider view of the west end of Waverley on 27 May 1981 the massive North British Hotel is the dominant feature with Class 40 No 40.148 leaving with a northbound parcels and 'Deltic' No 55.008 *The Green Howards*, just arrived with the 05.50 from Kings Cross, playing the supporting role. The entire track layout at Waverley was painfully rationalised when MAS signalling was introduced in the 1970s. *LAN*

Below: Taken from Carlton Hill this view of the east end of Waverley station on 27 May 1981 is full of interest. The departing HST is the 'Aberdonian', 10.25 Aberdeen-Kings Cross, and it is passing the east end Class 08 pilot and an abysmally filthy No 20.191 on an engineer's train. The redundant east end signalbox, now used as a permanent way cabin and store, is behind the front of the HST with the new Edinburgh signalling centre standing out on the extreme south of the railway complex above the Class 08. This centre now controls the ECML from North Fife to the English Border as well as most of the Carstairs and Glasgow routes. Note the two 'covered wagon' car carriers at the platform — the pioneers of the present extensive Motorail system. LAN

Left: Edinburgh Waverley station lies in a very convenient location in the bottom of the deep valley which scythes through the city centre, dominated by the North British Hotel, witness to halcyon days when rail was the most prestigious way to travel. Other imposing buildings can be seen in this picture of Class 27 No 27.010 making a brisk westerly departure on 23 May 1981 with the 12.48 to Perth, to connect there with a Glasgow to Inverness service. In the background the driver and guard of the 13.00 Glasgow Inter-City push-pull service chat through the window of the DTBSO (Driving Trailer Brake Second Open), whilst a Class 47/7 ticks over at the buffer stops at the rear of the train. To ensure that the guard is able to protect the rear of the train in the event of a failure in the steeply graded tunnel leaving Glasgow Queen Street it is the practice for these trains to always leave Glasgow locomotive first. *PJR*

Below: Under the overall roof of Waverley station an HST forming the 12.45 Edinburgh-Kings Cross awaits departure from the most northerly platform as another set, the 07.32 from Kings Cross, enters the station from Carlton Hill tunnel on 27 May 1981. *LAN*

Above: There are excellent opportunities for recording the intricacies of Millerhill marshalling yard from conveniently situated road bridges at both north and south ends of the yard. During the afternoon wagon load trains arrive from the various Scottish centres bringing traffic for overnight continuation and the locomotives return with traffic accumulated during the day for their home area. Here Gateshead allocated No 37.068 leaves the departure sidings with a light load for Perth and the Highland line on on Good Friday, 9 April 1982. *PJR*

Right: Millerhill TMD is the home of Class 26 Nos 26.001-7 which are fitted with two way radio and Slow Speed Control specifically for handling MGR coal traffic from Lothian collieries to Cockenzie and Longannet power stations and Leith docks (for shipment). The radio is necessary for certain 'blind' movements enabling the guard to pass instructions to the driver in locations where he cannot be seen. Here No 26.007 is cautiously negotiating the rural Bilston Glen branch, approaching Millerhill with MGR coal for Cockenzie power station. This branch was originally the ex-NBR Penicuik branch. Photographed on 14 June 1982. *PJR*

Above: The use of a 200mm lens highlights the variety of vehicles stabled in the east side of Millerhill yard, now used for staging complete trains and for stabling civil engineers vehicles. No 25.240 is running through the yard on tracks that were the erstwhile Waverley route which bisected the yard. Traffic is now handled in the west side into which No 25.240 will deliver its varied load of air braked vehicles from Leith after running round at the south end. Good Friday, 9 April 1982. *PJR*

Below: Most freight traffic beween Millerhill and points north and west of Edinburgh by-passes Waverley station by using the now freight only 'suburban' line which passes to the south of Arthur's Seat and joins the passenger lines at Haymarket. This is an interesting little loop punctuated at regular intervals by the island platforms of long closed stations. Here a 150mm lens is used to emphasise the bulk of Arthur's seat behind No 20.020 negotiating the junction at Niddrie — an evocative name for LNER devotees — on the approach to Millerhill at the eastern end of the 'Sub' with a remarkably uniform ballast train on 8 September 1980. *PJR*

Right: No 20.205 passes high above South Queensferry on the southern approach viaduct of the Forth Bridge with a ballast train composed of four-wheel 'Catfish' wagons. Judging by the dress of the 'human interest' there is the usual chill breeze blowing. 27 May 1981. *LAN*

Below: The line from Carstairs to Edinburgh is very much a challenge to railway photographers in view of the difficulty in finding interesting locations. There are one or two opportunities on the wooded curves around Dalmahoy on the western approach to Edinburgh where No 40.152 was caught on 28 August 1982 at the head of 1Z10, a Nelson-Edinburgh 'Tattoo' special. It was formed by the SLOA Pullman train which had been electrically hauled to Carstairs. *PJR*

Above: Against the forbidding background of Carstairs Hospital for the dangerously insane No 47.701 *Saint Andrew* takes a break from Edinburgh-Glasgow push-pull duties, to work the Edinburgh portion of the 12.05 from Birmingham which will have been detached from the rear of the main Glasgow portion at Carstairs. Photographed on 13 April 1979. *LAN*

Left: Formerly the route of the Glasgow-St Andrews 'Fife Coast Express' the Winchburgh Junction-Dalmeny connection between the Edinburgh and Glasgow and the Edinburgh-Aberdeen lines is now freight only. Here No 27.028 negotiates this stretch, having just passed under the M8 with a Glasgow (Queen Street) to Dunfermline Celtic football supporters special (1Z35) on 28 August 1982. *PJR*

Left: Glasgow (Queen Street) is a funeral terminus from which departing trains plunge off the platform end into a murky tunnel at the start of the $1\frac{1}{4}$-mile climb at 1 in 41 to Carstairs. Virtually no shunting is carried out, the incoming locomotive frequently banking the departing train up the bank. Here is a bird's-eye view of No 27.203, supported by a sister locomotive at the rear of the train, awaiting departure with the 14.00 push-pull Edinburgh train on 4 September 1977. *LAN*

Above right: The demolition of an overbridge north of Eastfield, Scotland's largest TMD, has opened up a splendid view of the North End of the depot as a background to northbound trains from Glasgow (Queen Street). Snow plough fitted No 26.025 regains the main line after detaching a banker in the loop, with 1Z43 18.20 Queen Street-Dundee return football excursion on the occasion of the Scotland v England match on 29 May 1982. *PJR*

Below right: For many years Sunday journeys over the West Coast main line have been considerably extended due to lengthy scheduled diversions to enable essential engineering work to be carried out on the electrified system. The impact on journey time is such that Glasgow to London passengers on Sundays are advised to travel via Edinburgh and the East Coast main line and a through HST service from Glasgow (Queen Street) to Kings Cross at 09.45 was introduced in 1981. This picture shows this train emerging from Queen Street tunnel into the desolation of Glasgow's 'inner city' as it forges up the 1 in 41 of Cowlairs bank on Sunday, 9 August 1981. *LAN*

Clyde Suburban

Above: Against the background of Dumbarton Castle standing guard over the industrial and residential sprawl of the town, a Class 303 scurries along the south bank of the Clyde near Langbank forming the 14.45 Gourock-Glasgow on 15 April 1982. *LAN*

Above right: In the city centre environment of Glasgow (Central) EMU No 303 055, forming the 14.40 to Wemyss Bay, glides quietly out of the most westerly platform of this huge, busy station, from which trains run immediately on to a multi-track bridge over the Clyde. Photographed on 4 September 1977. *LAN*

Below right: The extensive Clydeside suburban network was gradually electrified in the early 1960s when the 'Blue Trains', presently BR Class 303, were introduced taking power from 25kV overhead wires. After dramatic teething troubles involving their complete withdrawal for a while after some explosions in the switch gear they settled down to give some 20 years of reliable service. Arguably the most pleasing of all BR EMU designs in view of the rounded end contours and smooth sides with sliding doors they still do not look dated 20 years after being introduced. It is pleasing to note the distinctive Gresley bogies which were so successful on the ECML fliers still giving sterling service. Here unit No 303 021 leaves Balloch on Loch Lomond with the 16.00 to Springburn on 1 May 1982. It is difficult to think of a greater contrast than that between the scenic beauty of Loch Lomond at one end of this route and the urban dereliction of the Springburn area of Glasgow at the other. *PJR*

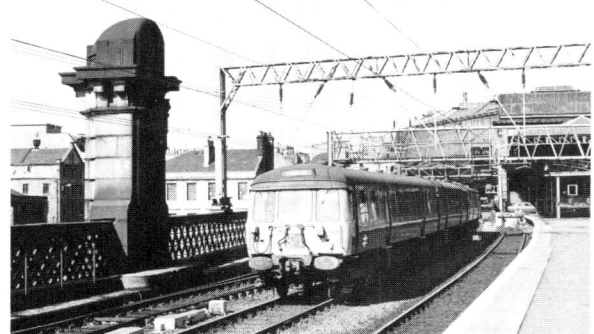

Above: Within 25min of leaving Glasgow, trains for Gourock and Wemyss Bay reach the attractive Clydeside scenery around Langbank with extensive and impressive views across the 'watter' to Helensburgh, and the mountains in the vicinity of Loch Lomond, before a return to the industrial depression of Port Glasgow and Greenock. Here two Class 303 units form the 10.45 Gourock-Glasgow on 15 April 1982. *LAN*

Below: Any romantic illusions evoked by the beautiful views across the Clyde at Langbank are shattered by the heavy industry of Port Glasgow in the midst of which a 'Blue Train' can just be seen heading for Wemyss Bay on 15 April 1982. *LAN*

Edinburgh-Glasgow

The peculiar operating requirements of the 47-mile Edinburgh-Glasgow service have resulted in the provision of unique rolling stock since through traffic between the two cities was concentrated on the ex-LNER Waverley to Queen Street route via Falkirk. The need for minimum journey and speedy turnround times seemed ideal for DMU operation and special vehicles including catering facilities replaced the previous steam services in 1956/7. In an attempt to improve journey times in 1971 these units gave way to six coach trains of open Mk 2a stock operated by two specially adapted Class 27 locomotives, one at each end. 24 such engines were provided, 12 push pull fitted designated Class 27/1 and a further 12 were both push pull and ETH fitted (Class 27/2) to provide train heating. This system operated successfully at speeds of up to 90mph until 1980, although towards the end of this period the maintenance depots at Haymarket and Eastfield were heavily occupied in keeping these ageing Type 2 locomotives serviceable on high speed duties for which they were not really designed.

However the innovation of a much simplified push-pull system operated through the lighting circuits facilitated the introduction of Mk 3 stock on this service in 1980, traction being provided by an adapted Class 47 (designated 47/7) locomotive at one end. A driving position at the other end was provided by converting eight Mk 2d BSOs to a Driving Trailer Brake Second Open (DTBSO). These trains have decidedly improved both the speed and reliability of service. The inspired initiative of bestowing upon the 12 Class 47/7s evocative names and maintaining them in good external condition has served to increase the attraction of the excellent half hourly service.

Below left: Shortly before the introduction of MAS signalling from the centralised Edinburgh box. Nos 27.206 and 27.102 (at rear) hammer along at 90mph near Linlithgow with the 13.30 Edinburgh to Glasgow on 3 October 1978. Note the outline of both Forth Bridges on the skyline. *PJR*

Below: The high speed push-pull trains take the direct route between Polmont and Greenhill through Falkirk (High) overtaking in the process, slower DMU operated stopping trains via Falkirk (Grahamston). Here Nos 27.102 and 27.110 (at the rear) approach the tunnel at Falkirk (High) with the 11.30 Edinburgh to Glasgow on 20 April 1979. *LAN*

Above: Very early on a misty June morning in 1981 No 47.712 *Lady Diana Spencer* hurries the 06.20 Glasgow-Edinburgh through Greenhill. The names for Nos 47.711 and 47.712 were decided by a ballot of suggestions to a Scottish newspaper, followed by public naming ceremonies. No 47.711 was named *Greyfriars Bobby* after the legendary terrier dog which maintained a 15-year vigil by the grave of its owner in Greyfriars cemetery, Edinburgh. *LAN*

Below: On Sundays Edinburgh and Glasgow services run semi-fast via Falkirk (Grahamston) where No 47.711 is seen with the 12.00 Glasgow-Edinburgh on 26 August 1980. During 1980 extensive repairs were needed to the tunnel on the direct route and for several weeks all trains ran via Grahamston. *LAN*

Edinburgh-Glasgow Diversion

Left and below left: Over the 1982 Easter
holiday, all trains between Edinburgh and
Glasgow were diverted over the
ex-Caledonian line via Shotts terminating at
Glasgow (Central) because of bridge works at
Linlithgow. This is a much more sinuous and
undulating line as can be seen from these
two pictures of No 47.710 *Sir Walter Scott*
propelling the 13.30 Glasgow Central-
Edinburgh service uphill near Hartwood on
11 April 1982. Although this route is still
open to passenger traffic, the DMU service is
very slow, maintaining a local service at
roughly two hourly intervals with an overall
journey time of 93min compared with
44-47min via Falkirk.   *PJR*

Right: Propelled by No 47.705 *Lothian*, the
diverted 15.30 Glasgow (Central)-Edinburgh
passes through the deep cutting between
Carfin and Cleland on 11 April 1982.   *LAN*

Below: No 47.712 *Lady Diana Spencer*
finds herself under unaccustomed overhead
25kV wires passing Polmadie and heading
for Glasgow Central with the diverted 16.00
from Edinburgh on 11 April 1982.   *LAN*

Above: The higher ground traversed by the Shotts route is bleak and inhospitable as can be seen from this picture of No 37.154 passing the windswept community of Fauldhouse with eastbound ECS on 10 April 1982. *LAN*

Below: There is a complex of junctions at Greenhill where the ex-Caledonian lines from Glasgow and Carlisle to Perth and the north meet the Edinburgh and Glasgow line. Without reversal there is no access to the ex-CR line from the line *from* Falkirk (High). Here No 25.057 with Craigentinny to Cumbernauld ECS to form 1Z21 10.30 Cumbernauld to Corkerhill Papal visit special leaves the line from Falkirk Grahamston to soon pass underneath it up the Sma' Glen to Cumbernauld on 1 June 1982. *LAN*

Right: Since 1981 BR have been moving a large shale oil spoil 'Bing' from Deans near Livingston to Carmyle in central Glasgow. Routed via Shotts on weekdays, these trains run via Falkirk and Cumbernauld on Sundays when their normal line is closed. They are worked by pairs of Class 20 locomotives, using 24-ton hoppers formerly used for coal traffic. Here Nos 20.101 and 20.028 struggle at a walking pace up the Sma' Glen at Cumbernauld on Sunday 13 June 1982. This sylvan location is in the centre of the new town of Cumbernauld. *PJR*

Fife

This is another area which has lost a significant amount of track mileage, the most noteworthy closures being the line from Cowdenbeath to Perth via Glenfarg and that from Thornton Junction round the coast to St Andrews. Whilst Fife has no really dramatic scenery there are some picturesque stretches between Inverkeithing and Kirkcaldy on the coast to say nothing of the two major bridges over the Firths of Forth and Tay providing railway lifelines at the southerly and northerly extremities respectively. There is substantial long distance passenger business over the East Coast main line to and from the oil boom centres of Aberdeen and Dundee, and this route also carries appreciable commuter and shopping traffic to Edinburgh. This is catered for by hourly semi-fast services from Dundee interspersed with hourly stopping trains from Kirkcaldy to give a half hourly service thence to Edinburgh. While the Kirkcaldy trains remain DMU operated, the Dundee semi-fasts reverted to loco-haulage in October 1981, formed of four Mk 1 coaches powered by Type 2 locos of Classes 26 or 27 with occasional assistance from Class 47. In most cases loco and stock are older than the DMU vehicles they have displaced. On the freight side there is coal traffic in the south of the country and a wide variety of general freight conveyed by Speedlink Freightliner and vacuum braked services between Aberdeen, Dundee and Edinburgh.

Below: No collection of Scottish railway pictures would be complete without the Forth Bridge, arguably the most impressive railway bridge in the world. This view of 'Deltic' No 55.017 *Durham Light Infantry* heading the 08.55 Waverley–Aberdeen across the famous bridge into Fife on 20 April 1981 must be one of the best possible. Only in their last two years were the 'Deltics' seen occasionally north of Edinburgh.
Gavin Morrison

Above: Class 40 No 40.123 does not appear to be burning its fuel as efficiently as it should, as it struggles up the 1 in 70 after a stop at Inverkeithing with the 12.40 Inverness-Edinburgh on 20 April 1979. This train, which was discontinued in 1982, was routed from Perth over the single line branch to Ladybank. *LAN*

Left: With the cantilevers of the Forth Bridge on the skyline No 40.157 restarts from its call at Inverkeithing with the 15.12 Edinburgh-Inverness via Ladybank on 2 June 1979. *PJR*

Right: No 20.039 prepares to leave Oakley sidings with a load of coal from Comrie Colliery which it will trip to Townhill yard at Dunfermline, 4 June 1982. *LAN*

Below: This evocative picture of No 20.039 passing through the closed station at Dunfermline (Upper) shows just how tragically the British railway system has been allowed to atrophy. This line once carried a passenger service to Alloa and Stirling but now sees only infrequent mineral trains. Photographed on 4 June 1982. *LAN*

Above: An unidentified Class 27 opens up after the severe speed restriction through Burntisland station with the 11.17 Edinburgh–Dundee on 4 June 1982. The idle cranes in the dockyard, provide a useful balancing factor for the composition. *LAN*

Below: Taken from the road overbridge a few yards further north, the cranes can only just be seen unloading a mineral cargo from a visiting vessel, as a three-car DMU forming the 09.40 Edinburgh–Kirkaldy accelerates smokily away from its brief call at the station on 28 August 1982. *PJR*

Right: These days Aberdour must be a strong contender for the title of the most lovingly cared for station on British Rail. In addition to the beautiful gardens and spick and span buildings, the interior of the public rooms is scrupulously clean and polished. Well worth a visit in mid summer to revive memories of happier days for our railways. In this picture an immaculate Class 26, No 26.026, adds to the general air of well being as it rolls through Aberdour without stopping on 9 April 1982 with the 12.20 Dundee-Edinburgh. *PJR*

Below: A three-car DMU forming the 15.42 Edinburgh-Kirkcaldy approaches Burntisland, past the aluminium works, on 4 September 1982. *LAN*

58

Above: 'The old grey town by the sea.' Thomas Mann's description of Husum, on the Baltic is equally apt for Burntisland, here seen across the grassy links, playing host to the amusements of the annual fair, as No 27.037 makes a severe brake application in deference to the speed restriction through the curving station. Burntisland was chosen as the home for the LNER emergency control centre during World War 2. The huge concrete bunker constructed for his purpose still exists across the road from which this view of the 09.21 Dundee-Edinburgh was taken on 28 August 1982. *PJR*

Left: At the top of this picture, the delights of Burntisland are still clearly visible $2\frac{1}{2}$ miles away along the coast as No 47.408 passes a jumble of holiday chalets approaching Kinghorn with the 08.10 Newcastle-Aberdeen on 28 August 1982. *PJR*

Above: We make no apology for our apparent obsession with Burntisland as it abounds in opportunities for good railway pictures. Here No 27.037 has just passed through the station with the 16.21 Dundee-Edinburgh and can be seen against the background of the once busy docks. The layout of the houses was presumably finalised before modern planning criteria was in force. Photographed in September 1982. *LAN*

Below: For a short distance between Kinghorn and Kirkcaldy the line runs along the coast in a northerly direction making it possible to take sunlit pictures from the landward side in late afternoon and evening. Here we see Nos 26.024 and 26.044 scurrying home to Inverness with the 17.50 from Edinburgh which will reach Perth over the single line from Ladybank. On the bright, clear, blustery 23 May 1981, Edinburgh can be seen across the choppy Firth of Forth hardly justifying Sir Walter Scott's epithet of 'Auld Reekie'. *PJR*

Top left: In the comparative boom of 1980 severe overcrowding was experienced on the Aberdeen-Kings Cross services following shorter journey times and improved frequencies as a result of the introduction of the popular HST sets. To partially solve this problem the 10.05 Kings Cross-York 'Deltic'-hauled semi-fast was extended, for the duration of the summer of 1980, to Edinburgh; and to balance the 14.11 York-Kings Cross started back at Dundee at 09.10. The stock for this train was brought down empty at 07.00 from Craigentinny to Dundee by the train engine and for the first and only time this provided a booked passenger working for a Class 55 north of Edinburgh. Here No 55.012 *Crepello* sporting the Finsbury Park trademark of white cab window surrounds leaves the Tay Bridge with the 09.10 Dundee-London on 13 September 1980. *PJR*

Centre left: Forming the 13.25 Edinburgh-Dundee a mixed three-car DMU approaches the Firth of Tay at St Fort on 12 September 1980. Judging by the make-up of this train, the replacement of DMUs by locomotive-hauled trains 12 months later was not a day too soon. *PJR*

Bottom left: With Dundee on the north side of the Firth of Tay in cloud shadow, No 25.078 with the evening Dundee-Millerhill partially fitted freight climbs away from the Tay Bridge through golden fields of stubble on 5 September 1980. *PJR*

Below: During the 1960s and 1970s the lumbering 133-ton English Electric Type 4s (now Class 40) bore the brunt of the Edinburgh-Aberdeen expresses, giving way over the last three years to newly introduced HST services and Class 47-hauled Mk 2 ETH stock. In 1981 the last Scottish survivors were transferred away to more mundane duties in north-west England, leaving Haymarket with no Class 40s for the first time in over 20 years. One of the last to have a heavy overhaul was No 40.148 seen here, not long out of Crewe works, throbbing away from the Tay Bridge through Wormit at the head of the 14.40 Aberdeen-Edinburgh on 12 September 1980. *PJR*

Stirling to Inverness

The former Highland main line south of Inverness to Stanley Junction and the natural continuation south through Perth to Stirling with Caledonian metals forms the natural backbone of the rail network of Northern Scotland. Time was when lines ran west to Aberfeldy, Creiff, Oban and Loch Lomond; east to Forres, Keith, Forfar, Dundee and Fife. Even though few of these remain, this main line, particularly south of Perth, is still of fundamental importance to the modern Scottish rail network. The sections north and south of Stanley Junction are in sharp contrast in almost every respect. The double track CR line threads some of the finest farming country in Scotland, is relatively easily graded and is appropriate to the modern Inter-City service in every way. To the north of Pitlochry the predominantly single line has to come to terms with some of the most demanding terrain in the British Isles. The long northbound and southbound climbs to the summits at Drumochter (1,484ft) south of Aviemore and

Below: The signal gantry at the south end of Stirling station marks the end of the journey for English Electric Type 4 No 40.015, formerly named *Aquatania*, at the head of a northbound Motorail service on 1 June 1982. The track into the old steam shed to the left of the picture is still in situ although the building was demolished many years ago. *LAN*

at Slochd (1,315ft) south of Inverness are demanding propositions even for modern diesel-electric power. Drumochter has the distinction of being the highest point of British Rail which is reached by service passenger trains. Travellers over the route might therefore be excused for expecting to be delighted by some of the grandest mountain scenery Scotland has to offer, but scenically the line is rather a disappointment. In recent years an interesting development has been the extension of the mid-section double track from Blair Atholl through to Dalwhinnie even though present day traffic is well within the limitations of a single track route.

Left: On a warm and sunny summer afternoon Class 47 No 47.435 brings the down 'Clansman' (10.00 Euston-Inverness) into Stirling on 1 June 1982. On the right Class 40 No 40.015 rests in the bay after arriving some 40min earlier with the corresponding Motorail train from Euston. A short walk reunites passengers with their vehicles. One wonders whether the attractively painted tyres on the platform are some subtle BR advertising ploy! *LAN*

Below: A most unusual combination of motive power for the up 'Clansman', seen leaving Stirling behind Class 37 No 37.144 and Class 47 No 47.546 on 1 June 1982. Since the train was running almost two hours late it was presumed that the Brush had suffered a partial or complete engine failure. *LAN*

Top: It is interesting to compare this picture with the one above which was taken 16 years later from the bridge seen just above the Class 27. Alas the semaphore signals, the crossover and the former Caledonian signalbox have long since disappeared. The down station building at Kinbuck, now a private residence, is visible to the left of the brakevan. Class 20 No 20.138 reaches level track after the long six-mile northbound climb from Corton on 3 June 1982. In the late 1960s some of the finest performances of the then ageing 'A4' steam locomotives on the three hourly Glasgow-Aberdeen expresses were recorded on this stretch of line through Gleneagles to Hilton Junction. *LAN*

Above: The signalman at Kinbuck prepares to lower his up semaphore signals as an Aberdeen-Glasgow (Buchanan Street) express races by behind Class 24 No D5123 and an unidentified Class 27 on a dull day in June 1966. *LAN*

Above: The former Caledonian route along Strath Earn from Stirling to Perth passes through some of the finest farming land in Scotland and is today British Rail's most important link with the north and the north-east of Scotland. The stretches between Kinbuck and Blackford and between Gleneagles and Hilton Junction have, over the years, been the locations of many a spirited high performance run. Here a Class 47 approaches Greenloaning with the 19.25 Glasgow (Queen Street)-Dundee on 2 June 1982. *LAN*

Below: In 1982 one of the highlights for modern traction enthusiasts in Scotland was the 10.38 Glasgow (Queen Street)-Perth and the balancing 12.28 return working. These trains were invariably powered by a locomotive recently outshopped from Cowlairs Works along with a second locomotive coupled inside in case of emergencies. An interesting combination photographed between Dunblane and Kinbuck on 2 June 1982 was an immaculate Class 26 No 26.005 leading Class 27 No 27.103. *LAN*

Right: Until 1912 Gleneagles station was known at Crieff Junction and although the line to Crieff and Balquhidder has long since been lifted the station continues to enjoy a new disproportionate train service. In the summer of 1982 a weekday service of no fewer than 20 trains was offered for patrons of the famous Gleneagles Hotel and the residents of the nearby small town of Auchterarder. The station has been little altered over the years and visitors can appreciate the lavish appointment once provided by the Caledonian Railway. However the bookstall now remains closed and one suspects it is many years since these display stands were adorned by ornamental shrubs and flowers. Glimpsed through the window is push-pull fitted No 47.701 *Saint Andrew* approaching with the 08.38 Glasgow (Queen Street)-Perth on 4 September 1982. *LAN*

Below: A moment of intense activity at Auchterarder on 15 June 1982. Class 47 No 47.414 races through on the climb to Gleneagles with the 07.45 Aberdeen-Euston; Class 25 No 258 shunts the yard on the down side while an unidentified sister locomotive waits to complete its shunting movements before proceeding with a Perth-Millerhill freight. *PJR*

Left: Another photograph of the four-coach 10.38 Glasgow (Queen Street)-Perth approaching Gleneagles, this time behind ex-works BRCW Class 27 No 27.040 and standby Class 47 No 47.206 on 15 June 1982. *PJR*

Below: The Class 37s have not been regular performers on passenger duties on the Stirling-Inverness line but they are occasionally requested as motive power for enthusiast excursions. The northbound ARPC excursion, the 'Strathspey Explorer', with No 37.012 *Loch Rannoch* in charge, sweeps round the curves between Blackford and Gleneagles on 4 September 1982. Note the snowploughs and the West Highland 'Scottie' emblem beneath the nameplate. *LAN*

Above: In the 1960s and early 1970s the North British Type 2 diesel-electrics were synonymous with secondary passenger and freight duties in Scotland. One particularly interesting turn for many years was an afternoon fish train south from Aberdeen via Forfar. Much to the chagrin of steam photographers at the time the train was frequently double-headed by diesel and steam. A somewhat bizaare combination, an NB Type 2 and 'A4' 4-6-2 No 60026 *Miles Beevor*, was caught by the camera proceeding light engine through the station at Perth on 28 May 1966. *LAN*

Below: A sight to quicken the pulse of any modern traction enthusiast. Both in early green livery Class 26, then numbered D5321, and Class 40 No D324 double-head a Glasgow to Aberdeen express past Hilton Junction signalbox in the summer of 1965. The lines seen diverging to the left of the picture are the former North British link on the south bank of the Tay between Perth and Ladybank. The continued future of this line is at present in some considerable doubt.

North of Perth

Below: Killiecrankie is a mandatory stop for most tourists visiting Perthshire. A stroll through the woods takes them to the site of the famous Soldier's Leap, with tantalising glimpses of the railway en route. This sylvan setting for No 47.197 northbound for Inverness on 28 May 1981 is in marked contrast to the stark and barren landscapes 20 miles to the north at Delanroach and Dalnaspidal. *LAN*

Right: A lineside location which emphasises the fine architectural features of Killiecrankie viaduct. Class 47 No 47.428 heads south with the 12.40 Inverness-Edinburgh on 3 June 1981. *LAN*

Below: Class 26 No 26.025 leaves Blair Atholl southbound with a ballast train comprising eight loaded 'Sea Lion' bogie wagons on 28 May 1981. Note the attractive castellated masonry gateways to the bridge over the River Garry. *LAN*

Above: To the crews of northbound trains Blair Atholl is rather more than just another station on the Highland main line. In steam days a pilot locomotive or a banker would be attached for the long 17-mile gruelling climb to the 1,484ft summit at Drumochter. Even today the disused steam shed still stands on the west side of the line to the north of the station. Class 40 No 40.022 approaches Blair Atholl at the head of an attractive mixed freight bound for Inverness on 28 May 1981. *LAN*

Below: The whisky distillery at Dalwhinnie is a familiar landmark to both road and rail travellers in south Inverness-shire. At an altitude of 1,300ft the blizzards and snowdrifts of a Scottish winter frequently close the nearby A9 trunkroad and disrupt rail services. Judging by the location of the somewhat dilapidated snow fences the bad weather usually comes from the east! These days the stalwart of Highland motive power is the ubiquitous Brush Type 4; here No 47.421 continues the descent to Kingussie with the 22.40 Euston-Inverness sleeper on 8 September 1982. *LAN*

Above: An old pack horse bridge three miles to the north of Dalwhinnie provides an interesting and complementary foreground to Class 47 No 47.426 with the 09.45 Edinburgh-Inverness on 28 May 1981. Crash barriers of the present day A9 road can be seen to the left of the locomotive. *LAN*

Below: Without doubt the climbs at 1 in 60 north or soutbound to Slochd summit continue to command the respect of even the most modern motive power. In this scene the driver will have been easing back the throttle of Class 47 No 47.102 as it topped the 1,315ft summit with the 14.48 Inverness-Glasgow (Queen Street) on 29 May 1981. The alignments of both the new and old A9 roads are clearly visible. *LAN*

Top and above: Two views of the attractive eight arch stone viaduct 1½ miles to the south of Slochd summit at Slochd hamlet. No 47.467 eases her eleven coach train, the 10.35 Inverness-Euston down the hill and over the viaduct on 29 May 1981. Some indication of the severity of the climb may be judged by the fact that the summit is located in the vee of the hills above and to the right of the locomotive. On the date (picture above) the next train south was a freight headed by Class 27 No 27.042 but the majestic viaduct is almost hidden by trees in this view from the north-east side of the line. *LAN*

Above: For many years the Inverness-Edinburgh expresses were in the hands of Class 26s in tandem, a journey which requires every bit of their combined 2,320hp. Here Nos 26.026 and 26.046 bring the 12.40 departure from Inverness into a rain soaked Aviemore on 25 August 1980. *LAN*

Below: The main line to the south of Inverness is, for the first ¾-mile to Millburn Junction, also the route taken by trains for Elgin and Aberdeen. Amid an impressive array of gantries of semaphore signals Class 47 No 47.550, since named *University of Dundee*, approaches the junction with an afternoon express for Edinburgh via the Highland line on 31 May 1977. *LAN*

North-east Scotland

In total contrast to the Highland lines north of Inverness which are
featured later, north-east Scotland has borne the brunt of post
Beeching rail closures north of Edinburgh. In particular the route
mileage of the Great North of Scotland Railway has been decimated
almost to the point of extinction. North-west of Aberdeen the railway
has been reduced to a through route to Inverness utilising the former
GNS main line to Keith and HR metals thence to Elgin and Inverness.
Two GNS branches, Keith-Dufftown and Alves-Burghead survive for
freight only services. South of Aberdeen the closure in 1982 of the
final remnant of the Caledonian race track between Stanley Junction
and Kinnaber Junction was a sad event but one based on sound
economic judgement, bearing in mind its duplication of the North
British coastal route. The development of both Dundee and Aberdeen
to cater for the booming North Sea oil industry has promoted a more
vigorous interest in the north-east coast route. The introduction of
regular HST services to Edinburgh and the south, supported by some
push-pull Glasgow services operated by Class 47/7s has given the
area its best ever Inter-City services. As elsewhere freight traffic has
declined with significant reductions in the numbers of trains conveying
agricultural products, whisky and wagon load mineral traffic. Looking
to the long term future one wonders whether Aberdeen is destined to
ultimately become the northernmost outpost of British Rail.

Left: Class 47 No 47.147 finds 12 laden
coaches a relatively tough proposition as she
gets away from Aberdeen on the stiff climb at
1 in 96 to Ferryhill with the 10.35 for
Edinburgh on 3 September 1977. At the time
this photograph was taken there was no sign
of the new service depot and power
signalbox which were soon to be erected on
a site to the west of the line and south of the
station. *LAN*

Above: A Dundee scene which emphasises just how much the railways have changed since the mid-1960s. Class 40 No D363, under full power out of Tay Bridge station passes Dundee steam shed with a long train of Conflat containers in April 1965. *LAN*

Below: Somewhat surprisingly Dundee once boasted no fewer than three principal railway stations. Dundee East (a Caledonian and North British joint terminus), the Caledonian terminus at Dundee West and the North British station, Tay Bridge. Today only the through station remains, retaining its unique character of platforms located well below street level. The descent from the east is through Dock Street tunnel but here we see the western approach. On a very wet Sunday morning in September 1982 the driver clambers aboard Class 27 No 27.010 to start the engine in readiness for a 13.00 departure for Edinburgh. *LAN*

Top: When the Highland line is closed north of Perth the only alternative route to Inverness is via Dundee, Montrose, Aberdeen and Keith. Although such a circuitous journey (it involves an additional 82 miles) may be appreciated by the enthusiast, it rarely meets with the approval of the travelling public. In the pouring rain Nos 26.040 and 47.163 double-head the 09.35 Glasgow (Queen Street)-Aberdeen-Inverness into Dundee Tay Bridge on 5 September 1982. The modernisation of the signalling at Dundee is long overdue. *LAN*

Above: For many years the coaling tower of Dundee steam shed was a prominent landmark for rail travellers arriving from Perth or Fife. Here a Gloucester RCW Class 100 DMU forming a Tayport-Dundee service rolls downgrade off the Tay Bridge and past the monolithic structure on an April day in 1966. With the advent of the Tay road bridge the service was eventually withdrawn on 5 May 1969. *LAN*

Above left and above right: The remnant of the once prestigious Caledonian Railway's main line from Stanley Junction to Kinnaber Junction closed completely on 5 June 1982. The Angus Railway Group marked the sad occasion by organising two special passenger trains. A wreath is carefully placed on the front of Class 40 No 40.143 (above right) before making the final afternoon departure from Forfar for Perth. Earlier in the day the well filled six-coach train was photographed on the outward journey pottering through Alyth Junction. In the line's heyday express trains raced through here at speeds well over the mile a minute mark, (above left), indeed it was widely acknowledged as the race track of Scotland, almost level track with few major curves over the 45 miles from Stanley Junction to Kinnaber Junction. Certainly passengers would have had little opportunity to view the interesting rail layout here, with lines radiating to Alyth and to Dundee. Note the CR distant signal just visible beyond the end of the train. *LAN*

Below: No 40.143 runs round her train at Forfar in readiness for the penultimate departure for Perth. Forfar lost its regular passenger trains to Aberdeen and Perth on 9 September 1967 but the extensive facilities illustrate its importance as a railhead in days gone by. Prominent on the right of the picture is the bricked up remains of the four-road steam shed. *LAN*

Top: The single line section of the old North British line south of Montrose to Usan continues to be a bottleneck on the Dundee-Aberdeen main line. The curving 1½-mile stretch of track at a ruling gradient of 1 in 88½ crosses Montrose Basin at Inchbraoch with an impressive 16-arch red brick viaduct. An immaculate Class 40 No 40.151 needs all of her 2,000hp to get the nine-coach 12.40 Aberdeen-Edinburgh express on the move after a Montrose stop on 3 September 1980. *PJR*

Above: Recalling the halcyon days when Class 40s were entrusted with the haulage of Edinburgh-Aberdeen and Glasgow-Aberdeen expresses No 40.050 drifts down the bank from Ferryhill into Aberdeen on the last mile of her journey from Edinburgh on 2 September 1977. *LAN*

Above: On 1 September 1979 Class 47 No 47.422 takes the 16.30 Aberdeen-Edinburgh through the delightful series of gantries of semaphore signals which, until 1981, were the distinctive feature of the rail approach to Aberdeen. *LAN*

Below: The English Electric Type 4s were for many years the mainstays of power for the Aberdeen-Glasgow and Edinburgh-Glasgow expresses and it was commonplace to find several members of the class on shed at Aberdeen Ferryhill. On 6 September 1980 Class 40 Nos 40.067/086/160 pose in echelon for the camera. *LAN*

With Class 26 No 26.046 in charge the 15.42 'Up Postal' rounds the curve from Aberdeen Ferryhill towards Craiginches. Note the snowploughs even though the date was 3 September 1976; clearly the fitters at No 26.046's home depot believe in early preparation for the traumas of a Scottish winter! *LAN*

Above: Of the once extensive Great North of Scotland network the only major sections to survive are the Aberdeen-Keith and the Keith-Dufftown lines. The most recent casualty was the branch to Fraserburgh which diverged from the main line at Dyce Junction. The future of the main line to Keith seems assured since the two hourly Inter-City service is well patronised. Class 26 No 26.032 heads the usual five-coach consist forming the 09.50 ex-Aberdeen near Thainstone on 6 September 1982. *LAN*

Below: Years ago the workshops of the Great North of Scotland Railway were the major source of employment in the little town of Inverurie, 17 miles to the west of Aberdeen. Today Inverurie is just another station on the Aberdeen-Inverness Inter-City main line, but the principal station building has been little modernised and is a superb example of GNS architecture and appointment. A sizeable group of passengers greet No 26.034 and the first train of the day for Aberdeen, the 05.40 ex-Inverness, on 6 September 1982. Just visible on the right are the the remains of the bay platform which was once used by branch trains for Old Meldrum. *LAN*

Above: The Speyside area of north-east
Scotland is synonymous with whisky
distilleries and when many of these were
built in the 19th century a prime
consideration of location was the proximity of
a railway. Today few are dependent upon
British Rail although the Chivas distillery at
Keith is a pleasant exception. Indeed their
principal distribution centre is located on the
site of Keith steam shed and even utilises one
of the shed walls in one of the buildings. Each
weekday a whisky train leaves Keith at about
16.30 for Aberdeen. Here Class 27
No 27.109 rolls the train across a charming
Great North of Scotland viaduct near Huntly
on 7 September 1982. *LAN*

Left: A further, and almost identical, viaduct
is to be found just 300yd to the east and a
little later on the same day it is crossed by
Class 26 No 26.029 with the 15.50
Aberdeen-Inverness. *LAN*

Above: The photographer takes refuge from the pouring rain at Kennethmont as No 26.034 bustles by with the 12.40 Inverness-Aberdeen Inter-City service on 6 September 1982. The goods yard remains open to receive the occasional wagon of coal but the station was closed to passengers on 6 May 1968. Except for the seven-mile Kennethmont-Insch section, this 108-mile line is now single track throughout. *LAN*

Below: Boat of Brigg is a delightful location on the former Highland Railway Keith-Inverness line. As the name implies the principal features of interest are the bridges, one road and one rail, which span the River Spey. Both are steel structures and are clearly seen in this study of Class 27 No 27.021 westbound with the 11.50 Aberdeen-Inverness on 7 September 1982. Once over the bridge eastbound trains are faced with a formidable $2\frac{1}{2}$-mile climb at 1 in 60 to the station at Mulben. *LAN*

Left and below: The 11-mile long branch from Keith to Dufftown was once part of the Great North of Scotland inland route to Elgin in Morayshire. When passenger trains were finally withdrawn in 1968 the line was retained to serve whisky distilleries at Towiemore and Dufftown but freight traffic has subsequently declined to the point of extinction; presently an average of one train each week. On 7 September 1982 Class 25 No 25.072 travelled the full length of the branch; the train consist for the outward journey was one wagon of coal, for the return two empty coal wagons. Clearly statistics which would incur the displeasure of any self respecting accountant! The line is scenically most attractive particularly in the upper reaches of Strath Isla. In these contrasting scenes No 25.072 negotiates the tight curves and luxuriant trackside vegetation on the outskirts of Dufftown and (left) climbs steadily towards the summit at Loch Park on the return journey.   *LAN*

The Far North

Today British Rail's operation north of Inverness is perhaps the Cinderella activity of the Scottish Region; indeed it is this area which has suffered least from cutbacks and rationalisation. With the exception of the branches from Muir of Ord-Fortrose, Fodderty Junction-Strathpeffer, The Mound-Dornoch and Wick-Lybster, the system remains essentially as it was in the pre-grouping days of the Highland Railway. This may be surprising when considered in the light of the sparse population density of Argyll, Sutherland and Caithness but the vital transport role the railway plays during the depths of the Scottish winter must be acknowledged, even in 1983.

Below: Brisk business is apparently on offer at Inverness for the 17.20 departure to Wick and Thurso on 29 May 1981. Thanks to the development of new industries such as the UKAEA complex at Dounreay, the future of this, the most northerly line in Britain, seems assured. Indeed the patronage justifies the retention of buffet facilities on most trains on the more southerly sections of the line. The motive power is the customary Class 26, a type which has virtually monopolised these services for more than 20 years. *LAN*

The lines to Wick and Kyle of Lochalsh take their separate ways $18\frac{3}{4}$ miles from Inverness at Dingwall. Trains for Kyle almost immediately begin a gruelling climb at 1 in 50 to a summit at Ravens Rock whereas beyond, the line traverses pleasant wooded and arable country to Garve and to a further summit at Corriemuillie. The character of the line then begins to change progressively to the wild and barren mountain landscapes of the Highlands. The outward journey from Luib summit, 31 miles from Dingwall, marks the commencement of the most spectacular part of the line. The views of the sea lochs and the Isle of Skye at the western extremities are surely amongst the finest in the British Isles.

Scenically the Wick line is in marked contrast, although the seascapes seen from the train near Tain, Golspie and Port Gower are undeniably attractive. However for the first time rail traveller to the Far North, the lasting impressions will no doubt be formulated as the train trundles along, apparently for ever, over the flat, windswept and treeless Caithness plateau with just the occasional reference to civilisation at Kinbrace, Forsinard and Scotscalder. The economic futures of the two lines would also seem to be distinct. Passenger traffic to Kyle is seasonal and freight minimal whereas north of Dingwall both, by present day standards, are adequately patronised throughout the year.

Top: A line up of six Class 26s await their next turns of duty at Inverness shed on 29 May 1981. Just visible to the right of the picture is a Class 20, a type of locomotive which is an infrequent visitor to the Highland lines. The shed is uniquely located in a triangle to the north-east of the station. *LAN*

Above: Class 26 No 26.022 continues the journey to Inverness as it leaves Dingwall with the evening train from Kyle of Lochalsh on 30 May 1977. Just north of Dingwall is the junction of the Wick and Kyle lines. The seven-coach train, which unusually includes a Mk 2 1st, is much heavier than normal and was probably strengthened to cater for additional tourist traffic. *LAN*

Above: Garve, 10 miles from Dingwall on the Kyle line, is a particularly pleasant station which has changed little since steam days. Attractive features include the Highland wrought iron footbridge complete with oil lamps and the two signalboxes. The station which lies between Ravens Rock summit (458ft) to the east and Coriemoillie summit (429ft) to the west, is the nearest railhead to Ullapool and north-west Scotland. In the pouring rain No 26.037 leaves with the 17.45 Inverness-Kyle on 3 June 1977. Note the recess beneath the cab window of the Class 26 which once housed tablet exchanging equipment. *LAN*

Below: No 26.029 gathers speed as it begins the descent of Lairg Bank with the 06.15 Inverness-Wick on 2 June 1981. Prominent in the eight vehicle train consist are a number of BR standard BG bogie vans. *LAN*

Top: Class 26 No 26.036 takes the first southbound train of the day, the 05.30 Wick-Inverness, out of Rogart on 1 June 1981. *LAN*

Above: With a clear view through to Rogart station (seen in the middle distance) and the sea beyond, the camera catches the 11.45 Wick-Inverness with the inevitable Class 26 in charge at the start of the long $7\frac{1}{2}$-mile climb of Lairg Bank. *LAN*

Above: For locomotive crews the most important staging point on the Far North line is Lairg. Lairg is 67 miles north of Inverness and 94½ miles south of Wick and the usual crew changeover point. As can be seen, over the years a particularly effective routine has evolved , one no doubt born of necessity in extreme winter weather. No 26.024 on a southbound parcels train and sister locomotive No 26.031 on a northbound freight were photographed on 2 June 1981. *LAN*

Below: The last trains of the day at Brora. No 26.031, southbound with the 17.46 Wick-Inverness, waits for No 26.044 to clear section with the 17.20 Inverness-Wick on 2 June 1981. During 1982 some of the services on the Far North line were worked by English Electric Class 37s, they are expected to almost completely oust the Class 26s during 1983. *LAN*

Above: One locomotive is required at Georgemas Junction to work passenger and freight services down the branch to Thurso. The engine is usually changed by double-heading a north and southbound train on one day of each week which accounts for the pair of Class 26s, Nos 26.037/36, at the head of the 17.20 Inverness-Wick at Brora on 1 June 1981. *LAN*

Below: Class 26s Nos 26.036/7 double-head the 17.20 Inverness-Wick along the coast north of Golspie on 1 June 1981. Clearly visible above the fifth coach is Dunrobin Castle, the family home of the Duke of Sutherland. The construction of the line north to Wick was complete as far as Golspie by April 1868 but lack of funds prevented completion of the next seven miles to Brora. However in 1870 the third Duke financed the construction of the line to Helmsdale which was eventually reached in June 1871. In return the Duke was able to attach his own private coach to any train and he even had his own station, Dunrobin Halt and a short branch line built. *LAN*

Left: A face of British Rail which is in total contrast with the Southern Region commuter scene. The daily morning Inverness-Wick/Thurso pick-up freight with Class 26 No 26.031 in charge skirts the North Sea between Golspie and Port Gower on 2 June 1981. While this is a most attractive location on a sunny June day it must be desolate in the extreme in mid-winter. *LAN*

Above: Although the tiny station of Kinbrace only serves around a dozen farms and houses in the heart of the desolate Caithness plateau it enjoys a daily weekday service of no fewer than six trains. Here No 26.034 disturbs nothing more than a few sheep as it departs with the 09.34 to Wick and Thurso on 1 June 1977. *LAN*

Below: A familiar sight on the Kyle and Far North lines. The secondman and signalman/porter/stationmaster/general factotum at Forsinard exchange tablets on 1 June 1977. The locomotive is Class 26 No 26.021 and the train the daily Inverness-Wick freight. *LAN*

Below: No 26.022 rolls into Georgemas Junction with the 06.15 from Inverness on 2 June 1977. At this point trains divide, a further locomotive deals with the Thurso portion (the branch signal can be seen above the footbridge) whereas the train engine takes the remainder the $14\frac{1}{4}$ miles to the terminus at Wick. *LAN*

Bottom: Class 26 No 26.037 leaves Thurso with the 17.39 to Georgemas Junction and Inverness on 1 June 1977. It will take almost $4\frac{1}{2}$ hours for the 154-mile journey but at least in high summer the scenic journey will be completed in daylight. The unique Highland train shed and the former steam shed on the right are of particular interest. *LAN*

The Kyle Line

Left: A spectacular view of Loch Carron near Plockton. Class 24 No 5120 heads the morning Dingwall-Kyle freight on 10 June 1973. *John Cooper-Smith*

Above: In addition to the busy summer tourist traffic the Kyle line has, until recent years, carried a reasonable amount of freight traffic as shown in this picture of Class 24 No 5126 at the head of a train of two bogie and 19 four-wheel vans photographed near Duirnish on 2 June 1970. At its western extremity the line passes through some of the finest land and seascapes in Scotland with splendid views of Loch Carron and the Isles of Raasay, Scalpay and Skye. During the summer season an observation saloon is attached to the 10.40 Inverness-Kyle and the 17.10 return working. The supplementary fare of £2.00 is excellent value for money. *LAN*

Below: Passengers on the 17.50 Kyle-Inverness enjoy splendid views over the sea to the Isle of Skye on 5 June 1976. The motive power, seen in superb silhouette, is Class 26 No 26.025. The future of this 63½-mile branch continues to be the subject of debate and even diehard enthusiasts cannot be too optimistic about the eventual outcome. Without doubt the Achilles heel of the line is that it serves no sizeable centres of population. Passenger loading statistics for the long winter months must be depressing. *John Cooper-Smith*

Above: BRCW Class 26 No 26.043 climbs through spectacular Ross and Cromarty scenery at Glen Carron with the 11.08 Kyle of Lochalsh-Inverness on 30 May 1981. *LAN*

Below: The terminus at Kyle of Lochalsh is probably the most familiar rail scene in Northern Scotland. The Cuillin Hills of the Isle of Skye overlook Class 24 No 24.121 and the evening train for Inverness on Saturday 10 March 1973. *Gavin Morrison*

The driver eases the throttle of Class 26 No 26.031 on the eastbound approach to Achnashellach. This is one of a number of stations on the Kyle and Far North lines where, for certain trains, stops to set down and pick up passengers are made upon request only. *LAN*

The West Highland

The 164-mile rail journey from Glasgow to Mallaig is in our view the most dramatic and beautiful in Britain. Leaving the industry of Clydeside behind, the line climbs above the Gare Loch from Craigendoran and from there the remainder of the journey is a continual succession of glens, lochs, moors and mountains with the last few miles to Mallaig affording superb sea views of the Western Isles over the dazzling white sands of Morar. Trains for Oban use the ex-NBR line as far as Crianlarich where they take the spur down to the lower ex-CR line from Dunblane to Oban, closed as far as Crianlarich after a rock fall in Glen Ogle in 1965. Tragically these lines exist mainly on tourist revenue, the punitive fares driving the scattered local population on to the roads. Hopefully the subsidised users of various discounted Railcard fares appreciate the privilege.

Below: Class 27 No 27.032 hammers up the 1 in 60 climb of Glen Falloch with the 08.06 Glasgow-Oban on 8 April 1980 with snow still lying in the 'corries'. *LAN*

Train loads are now very light and the Class 37s, which replaced the Class 27 locomotives in 1981, after more than 15 years sterling service over the fierce gradients, are comfortable masters of the task. Freight traffic has suffered badly in the present recession, with the paper mill closed at Corpach resulting in the suspension of the associated timber trains from Crianlarich. To further compound the loss in business, the Fort William aluminium works has also virtually closed. Three or four freights a day are needed for the surviving traffic, comprising mainly oil, coal and china clay with some air-braked general merchandise van loads.

Below: No 27.111 reflects the evening light as it approaches Crianlarich with the 16.38 Glasgow-Fort William on an unsettled 9 April 1980. *David Nixon*

Bottom: BRCW Type 2 (now Class 27) No 5379 descends Glen Falloch between Crianlarich and Ardlui with the 16.15 Fort William-Glasgow on 31 May 1971. The beauty of this Glen is shown to full advantage in the light and shade of a clear late spring evening. *LAN*

Left: A telephoto lens is used to emphasise the majesty of Beinn Dorain (3,524ft) as No 37.108 climbs up from the famous horse-shoe curve towards Tyndrum summit with the 07.00 Mallaig-Glasgow on 12 April 1982. *LAN*

Top right: The long tradition of double-heading on the West Highland line continues, although almost entirely for operating convenience rather than because of the loads of the trains. Nos 27.042 and 27.014 are shown here at the typical West Highland island platform of Crianlarich with the six coach 17.44 Oban-Glasgow on 9 April 1980. *LAN*

Below right: Dieselisation of the West Highland line started shakily as the North British Type 2 locomotives which supplanted steam were very unreliable. Paradoxically one of these locomotives came the rescue of the 'Jacobite' rail tour run on 1 June 1963 to mark the end of steam power when the 'J37' pilot ran hot. Here is No D6137 assisting ex-NBR 4-4-0 No 256 *Glen Douglas* into Tulloch nearly midway down the descent from Rannoch Moor to sea level at Fort William. The fireman of the 4-4-0 is holding the tablet, ready to exchange it for the next section. *Gavin Morrison*

Below: No 27.111 runs into Crianlarich with the 07.00 Mallaig-Glasgow, taken from the now closed Lower station in which the track is retained for timber loading, although currently disused. Oban trains descend to the lower level over a spur running behind No 27.111 towards a junction about $\frac{1}{4}$-mile through the bridge, 10 April 1980. *LAN*

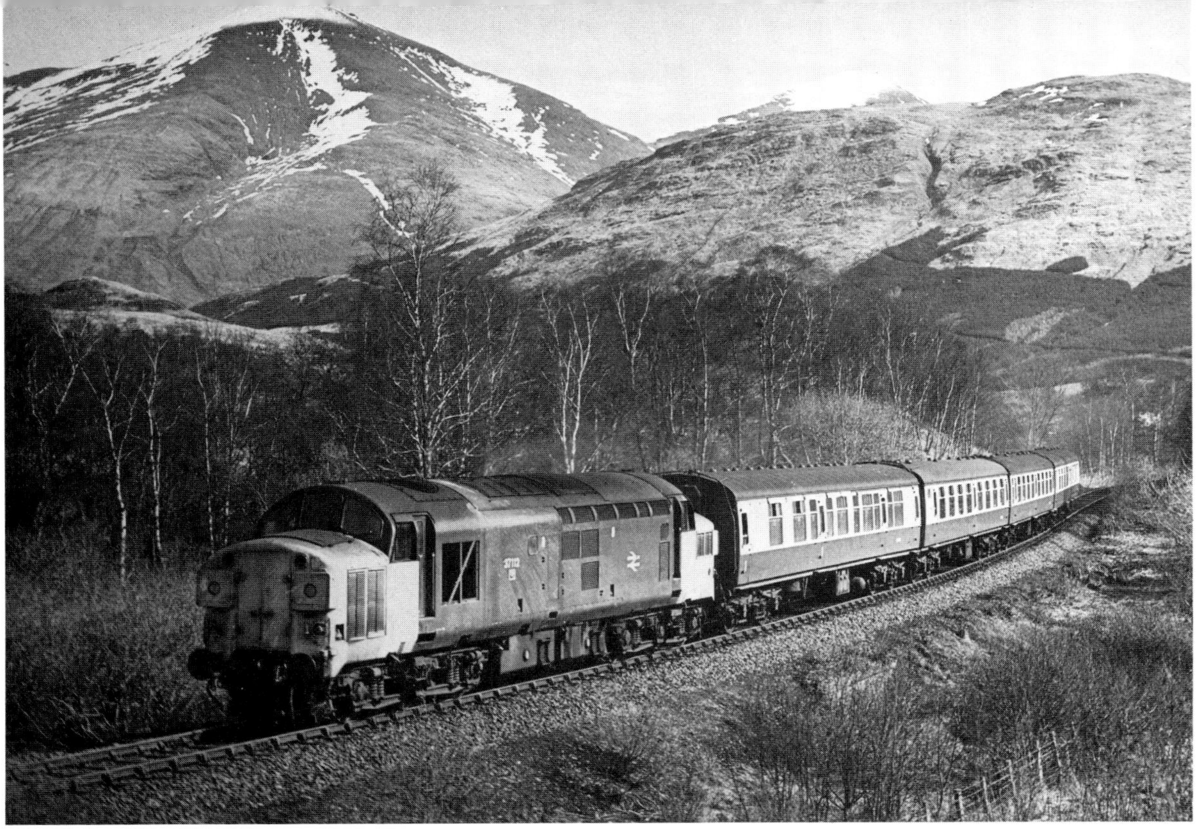

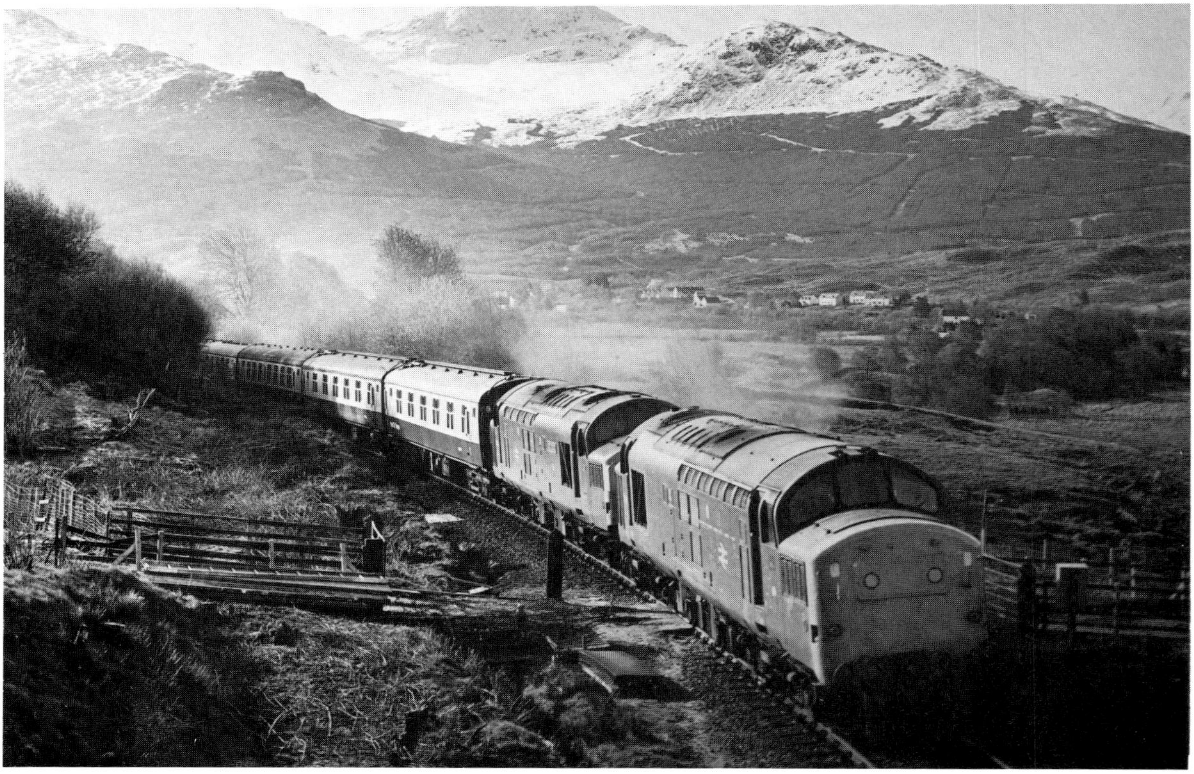

Left: With traces of snow on the peaks of Ben More (3,841ft) and Stob Binnein (3,821ft) No 37.112 sets off from Crianlarich towards Tyndrum Lower with the 12.54 Glasgow (Queen Street)-Oban on 13 April 1982. The West Highland line climbs sharply away from Crianlarich to Tyndrum (Upper) along the far side of the glen. Surely no one would disagree with our view that the 'new' BR livery is not suited to a Class 37, or any other locomotive with a 'nose'. *LAN*

Below left: It seems unlikely that any of the occupants of the two sleeping cars at the front of this train, the 06.00 Glasgow-Mallaig, have not been roused by the full-blooded exhaust roar of Nos 37.190 and 37.043 *Loch Lomond* as they do their utmost to recover 20min lateness up the 1 in 60 from Crianlarich to Tyndrum (Upper) past Inverhaggernie on 6 May 1982. The sleepers for Fort William have been detached from the 20.55 Euston-Inverness 'Royal Highlander' at Mossend and will return the same day on the 16.10 from Mallaig. *PJR*

Above right: The snow capped peaks of Beinn Dorain (3,524ft) and Beinn Odhar (2,948ft) look almost luminous in the crystal clear frosty morning air of 6 May 1982 as No 37.035 coasts downhill from Tyndrum (Lower) with the 07.40 Oban-Glasgow. An exceptionally late spell of wintry weather two days earlier closed roads in the area and played havoc with the lambing on local farms. The island platform of Tyndrum (Upper) can be seen at the lower edge of the forest in the top right. *PJR*

Below right: In the midst of the mountains No 37.111 negotiates the horse-shoe curve between Bridge of Orchy and Tyndrum at the head of the 07.00 Mallaig-Glasgow on 8 May 1982. Since dieselisation the lineside vegetation has not been checked by the frequent lineside fires caused by sparks emitted by steam locomotives. Before this shot could be taken without the intrusion of numerous bushes and small trees an energetic hour of pruning and cutting down was needed. *PJR*

Right: The old North British station at Fort William became a victim of a road by-pass scheme in the mid-1970s. It was totally demolished and a modern structure erected on a site $\frac{1}{2}$-mile to the north. This photograph shows the old atmosphere at the terminus on 10 March 1974. Class 27 No 5366 ejects a column of steam and exhaust as it eases back on to the stock of the evening train for Glasgow while sister locomotive No 5352 waits its next turn of duty.
John Cooper-Smith

Below: Britain's highest mountain, Ben Nevis (4,406ft), dominates an unidentified Class 27 running into Banavie with the 16.40 Fort William-Mallaig on 1 June 1971. This train is crossing the Great Glen before a lengthy run due west along the north shore of Loch Eil prior to the climb to Glenfinnan summit 17 miles ahead. *LAN*

This picture: Against an idylic background of snow capped peaks No 27.029 makes a welcome return to its old haunts as it climbs from Bridge of Orchy to Gortan passing loop amidst the wild Rannoch Moor, bringing the weed killing train on its annual visit on 7 May 1982. *PJR*

Above: After breasting Glenfinnan summit Mallaig-bound trains descend steeply to the level of Loch Eilt, the run along the inaccessible south shore of this loch affording magnificent views. Snow plough fitted No 37.192 is seen at the western end of Loch Eilt with the 08.30 Glasgow-Mallaig on 23 June 1982. In summer an observation saloon is attached to this train between Fort William and Mallaig, returning next to the engine on the 16.10 from Mallaig. *PJR*

Left: Proudly sporting its 'Scottie' dog logo No 37.027 *Loch Eil* bursts dramatically out of a tunnel through craggy rock on to the concrete viaduct over the head of the sea loch — Loch Nam Uanh — between Beasdale and Lochailort. Note the Thompson designed observation saloon named 'Lochaber' next to the engine. The train is the 16.10 Mallaig-Glasgow on 22 June 1980. *PJR*

Right: The extremely severe frost over the 1981/82 Christmas/Hogmanay holiday caused severe damage to many Scottish Region locomotives which could only be rectified by prolonged attention in main works during 1982. To our delight the absence of several Class 37s at Doncaster resulted in the provision of Class 20 No 20.191 to power the 16.30 Fort William-Mallaig and the 18.55 return on 22 and 23 June 1982. This picture, taken on 22 June from the rock above the tunnel, seen in the previous photograph, shows No 20.191 on the 16.30 from Fort William crossing the Loch Nam Uanh viaduct. *PJR*

Above: Mallaig, the terminus of the West Highland extension from Fort William is a sad shadow of halcyon days, handling no fish traffic now, the only freight being the occasional tank wagon of oil for the bunkers of the islands steamers and local fishing trawlers. This oil is conveyed as a 'tail load' on the 16.30 from Fort William, the empty tanks returning a day of two later on the 18.55 from Mallaig, probably the only 'mixed train' operation on BR today. Here No 20.191 has a tail load of two empty tanks as it makes a brisk start from a forlorn looking Mallaig, bereft of signals, with the 18.55 to Fort William, departing 15min late due to the late arrival of a steamer connection from Skye. *PJR*

Below: With the distant mountains of Lochaber shimmering in the haze of a beautiful summer evening No 20.191 scrambles up the 1 in 50 gradient from Morar to Arisaig with the late running 18.55 Mallaig-Fort William on 23 June 1982. In 1982 operation of the Mallaig line beyond Arisaig was changed to the 'one train in system' working, enabling the abolition of signalling on this stretch. This alteration makes it much more difficult to run additional trains to Mallaig — previously a popular destination for well patronised 'Merrymakers' from England. *PJR*

Left: On a glorious mid summer morning No 37.012 *Loch Rannoch* accelerates downhill after the severe speed restriction over Glen Finnan viaduct with its dramatic views of Loch Sheil to the south . This sharply curving viaduct was one of the earliest applications of pre-stressed concrete which looks rather drab compared with the more usual stone or brick construction. To generate interest in the West Highland line five Class 37s used as far as possible on Glasgow-Mallaig/Oban services have been named after appropriate Lochs following the previous tradition with Class K2 and K4 steam engines. These five locomotives are Nos 37.012 *Loch Rannoch*, 37.026 *Loch Awe*, 37.027 *Loch Eil*. 37.043 *Loch Lomond* and 37.081 *Loch Long*. They have further been personalised by a white painted outline of a 'Scottie' dog under the nameplate. *PJR*

Below: Early on a crystal clear June morning No 37.012 *Loch Rannoch* approaches Morar through beautiful dew-drenched countryside with the 07.00 Mallaig-Glasgow on 23 June 1982. The fixed distant signal protects the level crossing at the unstaffed Morar station, where the gates are opened and closed by the train crew. *PJR*

This picture: No 37.039 throbs uphill towards Tyndrum (Upper) with a maximum load of 10 loaded oil wagons — equivalent in weight to a 13-coach passenger train. Snow capped Ben More and Stob Binnein stand out against further storm clouds on 6 May 1982. *PJR*